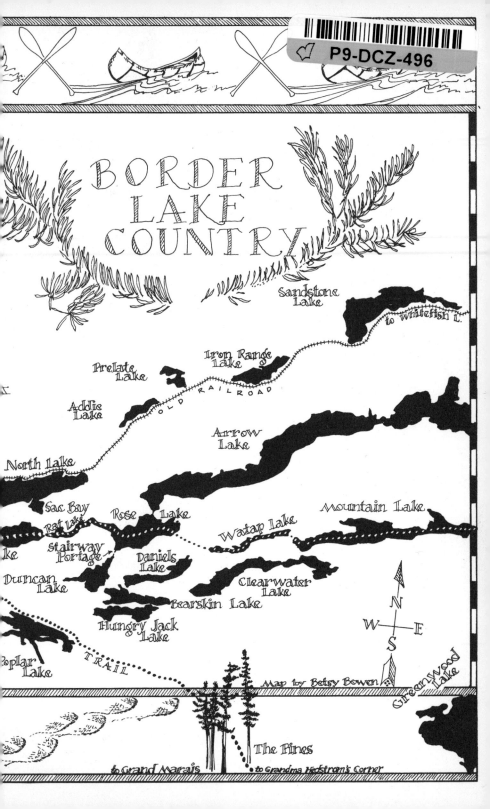

BORDER LAKE COUNTRY

Sandstone Lake

to Whitefish L.

Iron Range Lake

Prelate Lake

OLD RAILROAD

Addie Lake

Arrow Lake

North Lake

Sac Bay

Rose Lake

Mountain Lake

Rat Lake

Watap lake

Stairway Portage

Daniels Lake

Duncan Lake

Clearwater Lake

ke

Bearskin Lake

Hungry Jack Lake

N
W E
S

Poplar Lake

TRAIL

Map by Betsy Bowen

Greenwood Lake

The Pines

to Grand Marais

to Grandma Hedstrom's Corner

WOMAN
of the
BOUNDARY WATERS
Canoeing, Guiding, Mushing and Surviving

Justine Kerfoot

Foreword by Les Blacklock

Greetings
Justine Kerfoot 1991

Women's Times Publishing
Grand Marais, Minnesota

Grateful acknowledgment is made for use of the following material:

"Driving my Three-Dog Team, 1944" Wallace Kirkland, Life Magazine, © Time Inc.

"Charlie Boostrom" Steve Leonard.

"Early Snowmobile" Eleanor Matsis.

"Frank Powell's 'Standard'" Betsy Powell.

"Towing the Messhall, 1921" Charlie Cook.

Introduction of Justine from *Snowshoe Country*, p. 37, University of Minnesota Press, copyright 1944.

All drawings by Justine Kerfoot.
All maps by Betsy Bowen.
Editor: Jane Lind.

Distributed by Adventure Publications
Box 269, Cambridge, MN 55008

First Printing: May 1986.
Second Printing: May 1986.
Third Printing: Nov. 1986.
Fourth Printing: Nov. 1988.

Library of Congress Cataloging in Publication Data

Kerfoot, Justine, 1906-
    Woman of the Boundary Waters.

    Includes index.
    1. Kerfoot, Justine, 1906-   . 2. Boundary Waters
Canoe Area (Minn.)--Biography. 3. Natural history--
Minnesota--Boundary Waters Canoe Area. 4. Boundary
Waters Canoe Area (Minn.)--Social life and customs.
5. Outdoor life--Minnesota--Boundary Waters Canoe
Area. I. Title.
F612.B73K47 1986   977.6'75   86-4061
ISBN 0-910259-03-8

To
My northwoods friends
who taught me
the art of living in the forest and
the appreciation of all living things.

CONTENTS

   Strangers penetrate the wilderness. Canoe
   trip — what's that? City girl, moose hunter.

   The throb of the tom-tom echoes among
   the hills. Intermingling with our Indian
   neighbors. A birth. The rice harvest. In
   court. Illegal buyers. Christmas at Gunflint.
   My bitch meets a sled dog. Butchie's trapline.
   A dog team trip. Resort expansion.

   Learning to guide. Farm animals in the
   woods: chickens, a pig. A try at gardening.
   Consolidation and survival.

   Marriage. We build a log home. Diplomacy.
   Deer hunters, 1937. The wood supply.

Cooks. Gunflint Trail Telephone Associates.
Ice harvest. Light plant idiosyncrasies.
Plumbing. The Kerfeet Three. Children in
a remote wilderness.

ILLUSTRATIONS

FOREWORD

by Les Blacklock

I'VE known Justine Kerfoot for forty years. Actually, I've known "Just" for forty-*one* years. She's known me for forty.

I was in the army in the Philippines in World War II. I had asked my parents to send me a favorite book, *Canoe Country* by Florence and Lee Jaques. My folks not only did that but added *Snowshoe Country,* also by the Jaques.

And that's how I met Justine. The Jaques stayed at Kerfoots' Gunflint Lodge while writing and sketching *Snowshoe Country.* Two army friends and I read the book so many times we felt as if we knew Justine and Bill, Butchie, Bruce, Patty — everybody.

We were hooked. In a steaming jungle half-way around the world, we planned to visit Gunflint Lodge together, after the war was over. And we did, in mid March, 1946.

We had hoped for lots of snow and nice, early spring weather. And we got it. Beautiful blue days and crisp, northwoods nights.

Talk about living a dream! We stayed in the same cabin the Jaques had stayed in when they worked on *Snowshoe Country.* We got to know Justine and Bill, their children, their Chippewa friends — many of the characters in the book, in person. We ate with the Kerfoots in their log home, snowshoed with them to the cliff with its magnificent vista, rolled in the snow with sled dog pups.

Florence Jaques said it so well in the book, I'll let her introduce Justine. The Jaques were at Gunflint Lodge waiting

i

for Justine to come from Duluth. "We are all looking forward to Justine's arrival with much curiosity. We have heard that she looks like a 17-year-old boy, so much so that men are always mistaking her for Bill's son and acting accordingly, that she wears boys' shirts and pants, has a boy's love (and more knowledge than most men have) for motors and machinery, and a skill at profanity which a mere lad would find it difficult to match.

"Just before dinner last night, Bill and Justine came in with the two children. Justine is slim and dark, quite small. I had expected her to be a tall, husky person. Her hair was cropped short, she wore shirt and trousers, and Lee, coming in late, thought, in spite of all the warnings, that she *was* a boy, and looked around helplessly when Bill introduced him to Justine!"*

Fran and I honeymooned by canoe out of Gunflint in late October - early November, 1947. That crazy act in itself, so near to winter, may have won us points on Justine's scoreboard. We bought our wedding present to each other, a canoe, from Justine. On the bow seat she had painted in red, **To Fran from Les,** and on the stern seat, **To Les from Fran.** We were committed.

For many years I photographed Hamm's Beer advertising scenes in the Gunflint country, and gathered adventures and pictures there for several books.

I'd like to share a few memories which may help you know Justine better. I got this one from Fran. Before we were married, Fran worked at the Minneapolis Star and Tribune. Ed Shave, outdoor editor for the Tribune, told her that he and a bunch of cronies had been deer hunting out of Gunflint, and Justine was guiding them. Poor weather and bad luck kept them out a day or two longer than they

---

*From *Snowshoe Country*, by Florence Page Jaques with illustrations by Francis Lee Jaques, p. 37, Copyright 1944. Published by The University of Minnesota Press. Reprinted with permission.

had planned. And did they hear about *that!* Justine's mother tore into them the moment they returned to the resort. "What do you *mean* keeping a pregnant woman out in freezing weather? Can't you *see* she's about to give birth?"

There wasn't a gentler man alive than Ed Shave. He'd cry if someone smiled at him. So when confronted by this angry woman, he was nonplussed. After some hems and haws, the truth was finally stammered out. Not only were the hunters unaware of Justine's eighth-month condition, but until that very moment, did not even know she was a woman!

Justine probably enjoyed every red-faced stammer.

I REMEMBER —

Fran and I had fallen in love with the classic-point campsite, the tall cliffs and the great banner pines of Esther Lake. We were on our way to share Esther's beauty, her sparkling water and her loon songs with my parents. Our canoe was atop our car, and we stopped at Gunflint Lodge to pick up a second canoe for my folks. We expected that a Kerfoot employee would drive a second car and canoe to Sea Gull Lake and send us on our way. Justine had a better way. She grabbed an axe and headed for the woods. In a few minutes she was back with two aspen poles long enough to tie across our carrier and support two canoes side by side. A bit of clothesline and we *were* on our way, with no need to be met by another car when we returned to Sea Gull.

I REMEMBER —

I had never seen Justine in a dress. I doubted that she owned one. But here we were walking into a handsome Grand Marais church along with dozens of other people who were obviously dressed for a special occasion — Sharon Kerfoot's wedding. We couldn't help but be curious. Would Just be ill-at-ease, uncomfortable in this city-dressed crowd?

Not on your life! She could have *modeled* her outfit. Justine was a beautiful, charming woman with a warm smile and sparkling eyes, in every way a match for her lovely daughter.

I REMEMBER — so many facets of this woman — boy — hunter — poet — trapper — electrician — canoeist — naturalist — artist — zoologist — mechanic — writer — farmer — back-road world traveler — dogsled musher — storekeeper — guide — (gasp) — telephone line fixer — neighbor helper — stranger helper — beaver skinner — carpenter — woodcutter — story teller . . .

There is really no end to Justine's have-dones, can-does and could-does. I would not miss the mark by much if I said that Just can or could do just about anything she set her mind to.

Fran and I once watched, amazed, as Just paddled an otherwise empty canoe *up* a rapids with little apparent effort. No small trick; but that's Justine.

Like many of you, Fran and I have kept track of Justine and the Gunflint country through her weekly column, "On the Gunflint Trail," in the Cook County News-Herald, and through her Christmas letters. And, like many of you, when we were moved by Justine's poetic descriptions or exciting adventures, we would say, "This should be in a book!"

So we were elated when Just told us that she was going to do a book of her life at Gunflint Lake. How great it is to have so many experiences of Justine's wilderness life inside one cover. Now many more people can know Just, and enjoy and appreciate the north country through her colorful and candid writing.

L. B.

PREFACE

The purpose of this book is to portray a living chapter of history from 1927 to 1985. Although this record is based on my personal experiences they are not unique and have been experienced, to some degree, by those who lived in this north country over this span of time.

The encouragement given, by guests, neighbors and friends, to relate a few of my experiences over the past years has made it possible to present this material. To name these people individually would fill several pages. I am grateful to them all for their help and constructive suggestions. Special mention, however, is extended to Bruce and Sue Kerfoot who first spent hours editing and offering suggestions on the contents of the book and later worked to promote it; to "Chip" Wood who gave pertinent suggestions and encouragement; to Les and Fran Blacklock who emphasized the value of continuing my efforts so my relationship with the Indian neighbors would not be lost; to Barry Bonoff who opened the doors for book distribution; to Charlotte Merrick who furnished pictures and helped with the details; to Lois Mauck who typed notes so they were more legible; Eleanor Matsis who encouraged me to keep track of events for a future publication; Ade and Bertha Toftey who gave me the opportunity of practicing writing in their weekly paper the Cook County News-Herald, and of presenting facts realistically; finally to Jane Lind, owner of Women's Times Publishing, who was willing to gamble and had faith in the project. She worked untiringly to make this publication presentable.

INTRODUCTION

I don't know when I first knew I was in love with this sometimes harsh and demanding land. Did I fall in love in winter, when the snow is cold and crunchy as one pads along on snowshoes? When in the early morning the rising sun reflects on the hoar frost and each separate branch and tree in the woods stands as if covered with jewels? Then the fairyland is both cold and disinterested, yet somehow soft and beckoning. As I snowshoe across the lake, the wind stings my cheeks leaving them tinted glowing red. The snowshoes swish steadily over the crust in perfect rhythm with my swinging arms. My bouncing shadow, trotting faithfully beside me, imitates my every movement. As I rest a moment and look down the lake, the Sawtooth Mountains present a jagged outline, their slopes covered with timber and their cliff-like faces heavy with frost and snow.

Or did I fall in love when the change from winter to spring begins, and one hears the sound of the first gentle rain on the roof, running off in rivulets? As it splashes to the ground, it sends a shower of individual droplets in an arc onto the leaves and pine needles laid down the fall before. Mist rises from the ice on the lake, an impenetrable barrier that becomes a sheer veil moments later. Treetops on the far shore are suspended in an ethereal horizon. The ice rumbles, and a few seagulls talk their way across the sky, looking for a patch of open water.

As the days lengthen, a lead opens along the north shore of Gunflint Lake, and shallow bays throw back their winter cover. The sun melts the snow on the ice field, creating puddles that filter through the porous ice. The river melts little estuaries into the lake, allowing the wind to move in and push the monolithic covering, undulating, at first mere inches. The ice gives in, disintegrating into crystals or breaking into sheets that gain momentum as they move. Like miniature glaciers they pile onshore, standing docks on end or brushing them aside.

The snows melt. The sunny hillsides are loaded with small, sweet, wild strawberries; a few moments of picking produces a handful. The blossoms of moccasin flowers past their peak of bloom hang limp and brown like tiny pieces of chamois, interspersed in the woods with vivid red teaberry. Bunchberries gather in clusters, holding their white blossoms snugly against the leaves. Coral root stands stark and naked, leafless like Indian pipe, but showing a series of look-alike flowers that resemble minute orchids. The blooms of bushy labrador tea cover the marshy areas with a blanket of white. Red devil's paintbrush waves abundantly along the roadside. Ground pine spreads along the forest floor, holding its evergreen twigs erect in an effort to compete with its small, colorful neighbors. In secluded parts of the woods, hidden by overhanging flowers and large leaves, nests woven of twigs hold mottled brownish eggs. The evening grosbeaks, feeding on seeds and bugs, flash yellow among the dark spruce and balsam.

As fall approaches, leaves start to turn haphazardly, as if a child were dipping a brush in pots of yellow and red paint and dropping a plop here and there. It is the rutting season of the moose; bulls are in a restless mood as they search for mates. A flock of geese, chatting sociably, passes overhead at little more than treetop level. The mushrooms that come into being overnight carpet the woods floor with browns, yellows, reds and whites. These fungi grow rapidly, then spill their spores, shrivel and topple over. Beaver accumulate fresh food piles of aspen branches before their houses. Their nearby trails lead to trees chewed partially through, with fresh-smelling symmetrical chips at their bases. When the trees are felled by the first heavy wind, tiny chisel marks are left on the stumps.

Mountain ash is now a mixture of yellow and orange. Aspen and birch tipped with yellow and the deep red of moose maple are accentuated by the somber dark green of the pines. This is autumn's defiance, an orchestra reaching a crescendo, before the silence of winter descends.

I don't know when, but the fact remains that I did fall in love. An infinitesimal speck in the cosmos, I stood on the shore of Gunflint Lake beneath a great white pine — matriarch of a fast-vanishing tribe. And I knew I was home. I was 21. The year was 1927.

The Land

My life-long residency occupies but a fleeting moment in the millenia of the region's time.

Half a billion years ago, fissures opened and spewed lava, creating the series of uprisings now called the Sawtooth Mountains. Then came the glaciers. Twenty thousand years ago great ice sheets scoured away the loose soil and carved out basins of bare rock; wearing down the mountains of granite and greenstone. Eventually the ice receded releasing pressures on the crust. North-facing cliffs with trailing slopes to the south appeared as well as high gravel eskers resembling the meandering great Wall of China. The melting glaciers formed a shallow sea that covered the area. As the water ebbed Lake Superior was formed. Inland, a natural waterway was left, lake leading into lake, connected by running streams extending west to the English River and north to Hudson Bay.

The land became verdant. Lichen grew. Grasses and moss covered the rocky shores, building a rich humus soil. Fish inhabited the waters. Eventually a forest of pine, tall and stately, blanketed the earth's surface. Wildlife became abundant.

The south shore of Gunflint Lake was resplendent with white pines towering more than 100 feet, their tops spread protectively over the earth far below. On the north shore, Norway pines covered the steep hills, a solid army drawn up for inspection. The slowly-developing soil was carpeted with needles. Caribou moss was prevalent on moist, sunny rocks.

Mink, fisher, marten, lynx, wolverines, wolves and the migrating caribou made the timbered shores their home. Sporadically fires changed parts of the country, destroying some types of timber and allowing trembling aspen, jack pine, birch, spruce and balsam to grow.

The Voyageurs' Highway

A wandering Indian people, the Chippewa, followed the game migrations and made villages on these shores among the trees. From the trees, they fashioned canoes for travel along the natural highway of lakes and rivers and left birch trees scarred from the removal of bark. Portaging around falls and non-navigable rapids, they left beaten paths and campsites.

The waterway became known to explorers: Sieur de la Verendrye, searching for a northwest passage across the continent, was followed by traders and trappers. The French voyageurs brought song, laughter, romance and, to the Indians, white man's diseases — measles, smallpox and syphilis. They carried away furs to dress and decorate the people of the east coast and Europe. They left their mark with trade beads, clay pipes, pieces of flint, flintlock guns, shoe buckles and copper kettles lost in rapids, where their 25-foot canoes sometimes crashed and dumped their loads.

The Webster-Ashburton treaty of 1842 recognized the Voyageurs' Highway as the international boundary between the United States and Canada. The waterway and its portages were open to people of both nations. Trappers who already lived along this route were given exclusive trapping rights to their areas. They left for more remunerative work when the fur prices fluctuated and dropped. Their abandoned cabins and blazed trapping trails still mark the portages from lake to lake.

Rumors of minerals brought prospectors who worked their way inland, digging holes by hand. Traces of gold, silver, nickel and cobalt bestirred miners to enter this land of rocks and forests. But the veins were short, severed by the shifting earth's crust, and mining proved to be uneconomical. The miners, in their turn, left pits and holes of varying depths and miniature slag heaps over a vast area.

The timber, some stands hundreds of years old, was the next lure. Red-shirted, stag-trousered, caulk-booted loggers rivaled the voyageurs for hard, dangerous living and romance. The trees were felled, limbed, loaded on sledges and skidded along ice roads, hauled by multiple spans of horses. Once reaching a lake or river's edge, logs took the water highway to shipping ports.

The loggers left a far-reaching mark. Without the tall timber, the spring runoff was more rapid. Lightning struck the logged slashes and started fires that burned one way, then another at the whim of the wind, until they turned on themselves and were extinguished. Peat bogs smoldered all winter and flared up again in the spring. When the burned land replenished itself with grasses, small trees and underbrush, it was known as the bush country.

Then came others to fish, hunt, camp and canoe. Some stayed and built camps. A few of these neophyte resorts were sold to outsiders, and that is the moment in time when I entered the picture.

The Gunflint Trail

The Indians traveled an old winter trail by snowshoe and dog team from Gunflint Lake to an Indian village on Lake Superior. In places, the trail went over frozen lakes and portages to avoid the steep hills. From its origin at Gunflint Lake, it went up a gradual incline to Loon Lake, crossed the Laurentian Divide which sends water hurrying north toward Hudson Bay on one side and cascading to Lake Superior on the other, through several diversions and finally down the Sawtooth Mountain escarpment. Halfway along this 50-mile trail, Mr. and Mrs. Swamper Caribou lived on a lake which acquired their name. Their home was the overnight layover for dog teams en route to Grand Marais.

Travel in summer was more difficult. When a hardy prospector or trader coming from Lake Superior finally reached Gunflint Lake, he would light a fire as a signal. An Indian from across the lake would pick him up and deliver him to the hotel operated by Indians at the Canadian settlement they called Gunflint.

As miners and loggers needed to move supplies over the Sawtooth Mountain escarpment, the trail was improved. It followed the old Indian route in some parts, and in others, the roads leading to developing mine sites. A backwoods road was built with horse teams and hand labor, at the rate of 10-12 miles a year, until the road reached Gunflint Lake in 1892.

Improvements to the loggers' tote road, begun in 1917, made the beginnings of the 60-mile automobile road now known as the Gunflint Trail — although it was generally conceded then that no automobile could get over the hogbacks.

Over the years the Trail developed a personality of her own, as she followed the ridges, plunged into valleys and climbed hills. At times she made a circuitous bend to avoid disturbing a stately white pine. She was a humpity-dumpity trail. You suspected that at any turn she would squiggle out from under you and disappear under a stump.

The Early Gunflint Trail

Landmarks on the rocky and tortuous route acquired identifying names. At *Grandma Hedstrom's Corner,* the winter winds sometimes piled the snow 10 feet deep. Grandma Hedstrom with her daughter Lucille was there to offer coffee, a slice of fresh homemade bread, and the use of the telephone. The small clump of white pines at *The Pines* is a remnant of the trees that once covered the entire area. At one abrupt turn a young man on a motorcycle veered off the road and hit a tree; the site was named *Dead Man's Curve.* The frost holes on *McGinty's Knob,* just beyond Poplar Lake, became a quagmire with the spring breakup. These squashy boils changed positions as conditions changed each year.

Charlie Boostrom first came into the country in 1911. With his powerful dog team he hauled freight for forestry surveyors and worked for the Alger-Smith logging operation. Given an axe, he could build a house, a dog sled, a pair of canoe paddles, or almost any other essential for woods life. In 1914 he built a large log lodge four miles in on Clearwater Lake. He and his wife Petra brought fishermen and deer hunters to the area, and Charlie sometimes guided canoe trips through the wilderness.

Soon there were other lodges on the Gunflint Trail. Gateway Lodge on Hungry Jack Lake, one on Greenwood Lake eight miles by buckboard from the Trail and a small fishing camp on Gunflint Lake, called the Gunflint Lodge.

WOMAN
of the
BOUNDARY WATERS

Canoeing, Guiding, Mushing and Surviving

CHAPTER 1

"UP THE GUNFLINT TRAIL"

Strangers Penetrate the Wilderness

ON a mild midwinter day in 1930 while I was driving my dog team over the windswept ice of Gunflint Lake and carelessly sitting astride the upright crossbar of the sled, the team spotted a fox in the distance. The dogs picked up speed and raced across the snow closing the gap as the fox traveled at a teasing zigzag lope. The fox watched the approaching threat for a moment and suddenly became a blurred streak that left the team far in arrears. I was enjoying the speedy pace when the sled hit a hummock and tipped, flipping out my snowshoes which bounced like tumbleweeds tossed in the wind. I lost my balance and went skidding and sprawling across the ice. First the sled hung precariously on one runner like a ship floundering at sea then righted itself and sailed unguided down the lake propelled by exuberant and excited dogs. The fox was forgotten as the team picked up another scent and headed for the deepest bay. The dogs disappeared into the woods. I picked up my snowshoes and started the three-mile trek to retrieve and disengage the dogs from their entanglement among the trees. As I trudged down the lake I reminisced on the events that led me to driving dogs in this remote northern wilderness. It was a future I neither anticipated nor foresaw as I drove up the rollercoaster Gunflint Trail with Mother and a college friend in 1927.

3

Original Gunflint Lodge, 1927

Gunflint Lodge was a small fishing camp when Mother came to look it over. I had just finished my junior year at Northwestern University, and I was anxious to see what this country was like. While Mother and Dora Blankenburg, the owner, discussed purchase arrangements, my school-mate Mary and I made plans to take a canoe trip down the Pine-Granite River to Saganaga Lake and back. Although Mrs. Blankenburg had a few canoes, she had no camping equipment, so Art Smith, a local guide employed at the lodge, agreed to guide and furnish us with all our needs.

Canoe Trip — What's That?

Mary and I were excited over our first canoe trip. Art was an excellent canoeist as all the trappers were then. Our craft was a canvas-covered cedar canoe which was loaded, not on shore, but while floating on the water. When I first started paddling I lifted my paddle high out of the water, pulled with my lower arm instead of using it as a pivot and did not feather the blade. Art gave us some pointers. I was in the bow; he, of course, took the stern the entire trip. He emphasized to me the importance of a bow paddler who could pull the canoe one way or the other to avoid rocks. The stern paddler just follows the actions of the bow paddler, since he is better able to see the hazards ahead. I felt very important.

As I went down the first rapids I reached for one side and then the other, but in my anxiety to react I never wet the paddle. By the time I reached to avoid a rock in one direction there seemed to be a rock on the opposite side, and I'd swing toward that one. Art chuckled at my futile attempts; he knew the water well and could follow the course with no help at all.

Rapids on the Granite River

5

We traveled slowly and observed the wildlife along the shore. We looked at beaver houses and marveled at their construction, stopped for a leisurely lunch, listened to the call of the loon and "soaked up" the beauty of this remote waterway. Like the Indians, we followed the shoreline closely and observed everything: a beaver chewing quietly on a poplar twig; a blue heron standing motionless hoping to be unobserved; a kingfisher perched on an overhanging limb; droppings on a rock left by an otter.

Saganaga is 16 miles from Gunflint with eight portages of varying lengths; the longest a quarter of a mile. This is the same route, steeped in history, that the trappers, Indians, explorers and voyageurs had all traveled year after year. The country had recovered from fires that swept through in 1914 and 1918. At that time fires were left to burn; no attempts were made to put them out.

The first night we camped on Pine Lake.* At our chosen campsite a previous camper had built a bed of balsam boughs. It was made, not by clumping off branches and throwing them in a heap, but by breaking off new tips of branches and standing them upright. Small spruce logs were placed in an oblong border to contain the balsam tips. When the slow and laborious construction process was completed, the bed was like a cushion. Balsam was used, not spruce, because balsam needles grow only on the sides of limbs making them flat, while spruce needles grow all the way around twigs making them bristly.

Campsites always had birch bark, kindling and a pile of wood left by the previous camper, as well as a stack of

---

*The international survey maps denote the river from Magnetic Bay to Granite Lake as Pine River and the balance of the river to Saganaga as the Granite River. U.S. Forestry has since changed the name of Pine Lake to Clove Lake and called the entire waterway the Granite River.

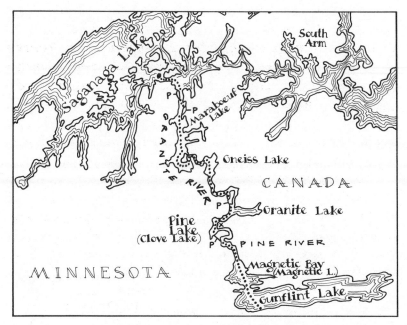

Route of the Canoe Trip to Saganaga

long slender poles made from the surrounding woods. These poles were used to support the A-shaped tents campers used then. When the camp was dismantled, the poles were stacked upright where they were found.

We paddled into a secluded bay, lifted over a beaver dam and found a narrow winding lane amid a floating bog. This miniature valley, flooded thanks to a beaver family who lived here at one time, was nestled between high rocky ledges covered with jack pine. We came upon an area where there were hundreds of pitcher plants. A few immature plants held their flowers tightly closed, while others were mature, with their pitchers filled with liquid. These mature plants turned their pale green faces toward the sun with their maroon petals framing the circle. Scattered among the pitcher plants were purple arethusa of the

7

orchid family. They had pale crinkled lavender tongues with center streaks of yellow partially capped with tiny shields with two slender petals attached. Three additional petals framed the flowers, like slender shocks of hair flapping and flopping with the slightest breeze. At the edge of the bog deep blue iris stood straight and erect in clumps. Along the shore were bushes of labrador tea with their clusters of white blossoms. Bull frogs emitted their drumlike sounds, conversing back and forth.

This narrow lane led to a small lake where we followed a protective cliff and watched the long shadows slide on the wake of the canoe. We passed a small hillside abundant with red bunchberries and a spruce that had toppled into the water with its top loaded with small purple cones. A spider had trussed the utmost tip to a nearby branch with its web.

We paddled out of the pond into another narrow waterway dotted with yellow water lilies. A loon was in command of this area, and by her actions we were sure a nest was nearby. We backed into a runway that led to an abandoned beaver house and waited for her to reveal the nest location. We silently waited and waited. She dove and emerged above and below us, letting out her shrill call. Within feet of us she sat upright in the water flapping her wings as if to exclaim, "what a boring game."

Art said, "We better go back and head for Saganaga."

We traveled but a short distance and we spotted the loon nest. Standing alone was a perfect cone, built of reeds and covered with sphagnum moss. The nest had a two-foot-diameter top and extended an equal distance above the water. In the depression of the cone lay one egg about four inches long, olive grey and speckled with black.

We returned to the border route. Upon arriving at Saganaga, we camped on an island and fished for lake trout.

Lake trout and northern pike were the only species of game fish found in these waters. Not until later years did the Game and Fish Department introduce smallmouth bass and walleyes into this area. Between the North Lake portage to the east and Swamp portage to the west, Saganaga acts as a huge basin, collecting water from springs, rivers and rivulets all along the boundary. Northern Light Lake with its tributaries is one of the big water systems on the Canadian side that feeds into Saganaga. All of Sag's water eventually spills over Silver Falls, flows north and northwest through Quetico Provincial Park, and finally, by way of the English River, into Hudson Bay.

When we camped on Saganaga, Art cut down a small tree to make room for our tent.

I said, "Gee, should we destroy a tree like that?"

And he replied, "Oh yeh, it will all grow up again and will be the same in another year or so."

On a future trip, maybe five years later, I camped at the same island and saw the mark where the tree had been severed. There was no new growth.

After several days of camping and paddling among the islands of Saganaga, we returned along the same route, for this was the only access to the border lakes. Traveling on our return trip was different, since we encountered the rapids paddling upstream. Art taught me how to ride the backwater and negotiate the fast water when approaching a portage. Art regaled us with stories of his trapping and hunting experiences as we paddled quietly across Gunflint to the lodge.

During our absence Mother had finalized the papers and made the down payment for the purchase of Gunflint Lodge. Prices were high, the stock market was soaring, and business looked very lucrative.

Mother had asked me, before obligating herself on a

purchase, if I would help her run the lodge in the summers. I readily agreed since Mother had largely financed my college education.

When we came the next summer, I had just finished college with a major in zoology and minors in chemistry and philosophy. I planned to take graduate work in parasitology and then hopefully go on to medical school. But before I returned to school Mother made arrangements for Art Smith to take me moose hunting the following fall.

City Girl, Moose Hunter

Moose hunting on the American side of the border had been closed for a number of years, so my moose hunting took place on the Canadian side of Mountain Lake. Art Smith, my guide, was to furnish everything including the use of his rifle — a .303 British. I purchased a Canadian hunting license, and Art contacted a girl in Grand Marais, Genevieve Bayle, who liked camping and was an experienced and able woodsperson to accompany me.

On a nippy late October day the three of us set off from Clearwater Lake in Art's square-stern canoe propelled by a small outboard motor. We made a six-mile trip down the lake to our first portage, the Mountain Lake portage of 88 rods. This portage had a substantial rise as it crossed a transverse ridge to Mountain Lake. Although inexperienced, I was anxious to prove my mettle to my new northwoods friends. We had packsacks filled with clothes and personal gear as well as sleeping bags, rifles and food.

We eased up to the dock and executed an expert landing. Art and Gene carefully stepped out. I stood up in the canoe and started heaving packs onto the dock. They both opened their mouths but, alas, it was too late. I heaved an extra-heavy pack, lost my balance and landed neckdeep in the icy water. My longjohns, wool pants, wool shirt, socks and boots were sodden and shapeless. Both Gene and Art had a difficult time containing their mirth at my awkwardness.

Gene dug in my pack and found my backup clothes: flannel pajamas and a pair of wool socks. From her pack she produced a windbreaker. From Art's pack appeared a bottle of straight gin. He filled a large camp-size cup to the brim and said, "Drink it." I dutifully downed the firewater and swished to the top of the hill carrying my scanty array of dry clothes. I stripped. The October wind held no mercy. As I redressed shivering, Art and Gene packed the guns, canoe, motor and week's supply of food over the portage. On the trip down Mountain Lake we faced a cold northeast wind, but I traveled impervious to the temperature with a warm inner glow.

Art's large log trapper's cabin was located in a protected bay. It was furnished with built-in bunks, a cook stove, an airtight wood stove, homemade table and stumps for chairs. These were common accouterments in trapping cabins throughout the north. If the cabin were a smaller, overnight affair, it might not have a cook stove; the airtight would be used in its stead. Traps, hide stretchers, axe, snowshoes, sleds, toboggans, saws and food staples were left in the cabin from one winter to the next. If travelers were ever in dire need and stayed at a trapping cabin, they were assured of dry wood and food. These items were always replaced in kind or with an acceptable substitute.

We strung my soggy clothes and hunting license across the room. The display emphasized my status as a novice.

During the week we were in this camp we saw 36 moose. Art remarked that in a few years the young growth would be too high to serve as good pasture and the moose would move on. His statement seemed unbelievable at the

11

time, but within five years only a scattering of moose remained. In some parts of the forest the moose herd declined due, according to the Game and Fish Dept., to a liver fluke disease which decimated a large number of animals. Their numbers were no doubt also affected by logging and the ensuing fires, as well as the decreased food supply.

The first day out I shot a bull moose. I moved in for the final kill and was confronted with a jammed gun and a thrashing animal. Art's large sturdy hand grabbed me by the shirt collar and pulled me back out of harm's way. The fatally wounded moose got up and strode off through an entanglement of windfalls. Art immediately started tracking the animal and moved way ahead of me. Instead of following Art closely as I should have done, I was tracking the moose in my own amateurish way. When I caught up with Art, the moose was lying down within sight on a nearby hill. Art turned and said, "Jesus Christ, where have you been? Shoot." One shot performed the coup de grace.

Me and My Moose

When we got to the moose, I was very anxious to help dress it out, cut it up and take an active part in carrying it the quarter mile down to the lake. Art said, "That's just fine with me. Lift up the hind leg and turn it on its back so we can gut it." I grabbed a rear leg and turned it, but nothing happened. I tried once more with the same result. I glanced up at Art to see him laughing gleefully.

A large moose weighs a thousand pounds, making it difficult to turn or move it. Art deftly gutted the moose, removed the heart and liver and skinned the critter. He

Packing out the Moose Head

left some hide on the neck attached to the head, because I wanted it mounted, as many sportsmen do. Gene, who had followed unobtrusively, now caught up with us. Together we surveyed the horrendous task of packing the moose through heavy brush the quarter mile to the lake.

I wanted to pack out the head with the rack attached; my friends graciously acquiesced. Carrying this head and rack on my shoulders and "bulling" through the brush was a challenge. The tongs of the rack caught on every upright stick. It is amazing how those animals go through brush with apparent ease, tipping their heads back to plow the sticks aside. We made many trips with packsacks carrying out the quartered moose, the hide, and even the feet — all of which

13

could be used. The job took the three of us two days.

We spent a few days at the cabin trapping snowshoe rabbits for food and hiking through the woods. We had to be careful on our return trip because in late October the lakes can skim over with ice very quickly. The newly-formed ice, when broken, is razor-sharp. If we plowed through this ice in our canvas-covered canoe we would likely slit the bow and sink rapidly. If we did encounter ice, we had to run the canoe up on the ice, shift our weight forward to break the ice, then shift our weight back and repeat the performance. But we could never safely use the lake equipment as an icebreaker.

We made a couple of trips down the lake from Art's cabin. Then we packed the moose and personal gear over the Mountain Lake portage and finally returned to Clearwater Lake. The mighty huntress had come back into civilization where people could o-o-o-h and a-a-a-h over the rack of horns and over the huntress' great ability.

In retrospect the recognition that we looked for from the public and the displaying of a mounted head on a wall were but moments of ego satisfaction. The head would have been much more beautiful if it were still attached to a live moose going through the country where it belonged.

An area that is heavily inhabited by moose has very few deer and vice versa. We took a couple extra days to hunt deer down near Art's cabin just east of North Lake where deer were more prevalent. I saw the white tail "flag" of several deer but reacted too slowly to shoot. On one occasion Art looked at me with disgust and said, "The deer ain't far from the tail."

On the way back to Gunflint from this expedition, we used Art's square-stern canoe and a motor. The wind picked up, and the water splashed against our clothing freezing on contact. We became almost solid sheets of ice; we could

Art Smith at his Cabin near North Lake

not move our heads or arms. Art pulled the canoe into shore so we could have a cup of tea and warm ourselves. The snow was now a foot or so deep, and I saw no way to build a fire. To me there seemed to be nothing but white bleakness. Gene scuffled around under the snow feeling for loose birch bark to collect. Art found some dead tree limbs, and in no time we had a big bonfire. We dried our clothes and warmed ourselves.

We beat the outside of the canoe to knock off the ice, and we were ready to continue up the lake and back to Gunflint.

CHAPTER 2

"EARLY DAYS"

The Throb of the Tom-Tom Echoes Among the Hills

WHEN I came to Gunflint Lake along this Minnesota-Ontario border, our closest neighbors were a half dozen Indian families living on the Canadian side of the lake. I listened to the low beat of a tom-tom reverberating across the lake on many afternoons and evenings. Billy Connors, a lone Indian tapping the drums, may have been dreaming of a lifestyle fast disappearing, or he may have been placating the evil spirit thought to be hiding in the depths of the Cow-O-Bob-E-Cock Narrows across the lake. The Indians

George Plummer, left, and Billy Connors Holding his Tom-Tom

paddled silently through these narrows "where the ledges come to-gether" to avoid disturbing this lurking spirit. That rhythmic beat of the tom-tom may have been Billy's final tribute to his vanishing race.

For a few years after my arrival, several Indian families continued to live on the Canadian side of the lake. The Plummer family included Netowance and her four children Walter, Gladys, Lillian (Butchie)*, and George Jr. Gladys, married to Pete Spoon, lived in a nearby cabin with her

*Lillian was known by her Indian name Awbutch but was affectionately called Butchie.

The Cow-O-Bob-E-Cock Narrows Leading into Magnetic Bay

17

three children. Mary Cook, a sister of Netowance Plummer, lived with her son Charlie. Abie, an older son of Mary's, married Bessie Blackjack and had several children.

They all had homes in close proximity to each other. This was a village of long standing, for on a knoll not far from Abie's house is a small Indian cemetery where several generations are buried. I went with Abie to this site when he buried his youngest child. A tick-a-noggin (an Indian cradleboard) hung from a tree branch. A few dishes and a can of tobacco had been placed at the head of old gravesites.

During the fur trading days, trappers and traders often lived with Indian women, produced families and then wandered on to new locations, leaving the families to fend for themselves. A few of the white men did stay, however, and learn the Indian ways.

So it was that Netowance, a Cree Indian, had "married" George Plummer Sr. 25 years before my arrival. Her sister Mary had "married" Charlie Cook Sr. at the same time.

George Plummer Sr. built a home and started a store and hotel on Gunflint Lake next to the Narrows (Cow-O-Bob-E-Cock) that opens into Magnetic Bay. Mr. Plummer dealt with prospectors, trappers and traders traveling through the area as well as with the neighboring Indians. Often he extended credit on food goods until the Indians had sold their furs. The price of fur dropped, and the Indians couldn't pay their obligations to Mr. Plummer. He went to Fort William to earn money to pay his creditors and never returned.

In the fall of 1914 Charlie Cook Sr. traveled to Grand Marais for winter supplies. In his absence, Mary Cook packed their personal gear and provisions for the family to make the annual move to their cabin on the east end of Winchell Lake. There they would hunt and trap through the winter.

While Mr. Cook was paddling down Loon Lake on his return from Grand Marais, someone shot a hole in his canoe and he drowned.

A few other Indian families were scattered on nearby lakes. Joe Blackjack with his wife and clan of youngsters lived on North Lake in a one-room log cabin with a dirt floor. Joe could only speak Ojibway and the youngsters, with no formal schooling, were very shy when they came to buy from our store. They feared they would be laughed at or not understood.

Eddie Burnside lived on Magnetic Bay with his wife and papoose. Mike Powell, Mike Deschampe, Ed and Billy Connors lived alternately on Gunflint and Saganaga Lakes, where the Powells and their in-laws had made their homes for a couple of generations. Mrs. Tamarack and Mrs. Spruce with their children returned to their former home on Gunflint Lake each summer where they erected and lived in two birchbark tepees close to the Plummer home. John Clark, a trapper married to an Indian woman in Grand Portage, had a cabin on the American side of the narrows.

Mrs. Spruce and Mrs. Tamarack at their
Summer Home across the Lake

19

*Mrs. Spruce and Mrs. Tamarack with their
Birchbark Tepee almost Completed*

*The Blackjack Family in Front of a Wigwam
that they Constructed*

These people were our neighbors. They became a part of our lives, for they shared unstintingly with us their knowledge of the woods. They taught us not only wood lore, but also the art of taking care of ourselves under adverse conditions which is basic to survival in the forest.

Walter Plummer

Many evenings a group of these Indians came across the lake and held a dance on the dock. The women formed a large circle and in time with the beat of the tom-tom they flicked their knees like a miniature curtsy and took a step. They asked me to join them, and I soon learned to make that slight bob from the knee while keeping my body erect and taking one step in a rhythmic sequence. Eddie Burnside sang Indian songs as he tapped his drum. On a few occasions the men brought over their feathered headdresses, wore their beaded vests and staged a war dance. Mike Deschampe, Pete Spoon, Charlie and Abie Cook were particularly adept in these maneuvers.

Walter Plummer taught me how to recanvas a canoe, how to steam and bend new ribs and how to make planking. Major repairs were necessary every other year on each canoe. In the spring I took the newly-canvassed canoes down to the dock and put them on a big scale. Each weighed about 70 pounds. By the end of summer, with the cedar soaking up moisture from rains and general use, each canoe would weigh 90-100 pounds.

The Indians would toss these canoes onto their shoulders with perfect ease and frequently trot, not walk, over a

21

portage at a methodical pace. For me to heave one of these canoes on my shoulders called for all the strength I possessed. The Indians taught me to use a tump line on long portages of a mile or more. The line extended from the sides of the canoe above the center thwart to, and over, the top of my head. If I walked quite erect, half of the weight would be on the tump line, and if I slumped very slightly the entire weight would be on my shoulders. By alternating in this manner I could go a long distance without stopping to rest.

The Indians utilized everything and wasted very little. They used birch bark for canoes, tepees and baskets. They showed me how to split spruce root to sew baskets. Pitch from spruce trees was melted to seam their canoes and sometimes used as a poultice on an infected cut. Deer hide was smoked for summer moccasins and moose hide for heavier winter moccasins. The men made snowshoe frames from ash or birch and the women laced the webbing of dried deer hide. Although I received repeated help in lacing a snowshoe, my results did not compare to those done by Netowance.

Gladys Spoon snared snowshoe rabbits, cut the hides into strips and sewed the strips end to end to form a long line that was wound into a ball. Gladys then wove this fur into a loosely-knit blanket which she presented to me as a gift. I could stick my fingers through its coarse weave, but it was extremely warm.

The Indians lived on the available guiding we had at the lodge in the summer, fur trapping in the winter and the fall gathering of wild rice. By trapping judiciously, the Indians and other scattered trappers could make a comfortable living, for their demands were simple. In 1927 there was an abundance of porcupine, snowshoe rabbits, partridge, skunk, mink, otter, beaver, fisher, pine marten, deer, moose and wolves.

A Catholic priest arrived one day and asked to be taken across the lake to contact the Indians. He wanted to convert them to his religion. He did make an impression on some of the younger people, but Netowance sat stoically to one side. Netowance told Walter later, "He has his religion, and I have mine."

Her spiritual needs were fulfilled where the sky, the stars, the woods and lakes became a cathedral. Helping neighbors in time of need replaced giving alms. The wind whispering or whipping through the trees, rain and lightning, and thunder echoing from one cliff to another, the crashing of waves against a rocky shore or the lengthening shadows on a still evening — all these replaced the words of a preacher from a pulpit. This philosophy slowly became a part of me too.

Intermingling with Our Indian Neighbors

In our little store we sold groceries to the Indians as had Mrs. Blankenburg before us. When the Indians came over to buy, they were unable to make change. They feared they might be gypped by these new owners, so their process was to buy one thing at a time: a can of snuff, a carton of milk or a pound of tea. They would put down a bill for one article, receive their change and go back and sit on the bench, count it, look at it and then come back and buy another article. Selling any amount of food to the Indians was a slow and long procedure. Now as I look back on that time I believe it was their social hour.

A Birth

Abie Cook came across the lake one summer day and said his wife Bessie was about to give birth to a baby. He asked, "You come?" I had never observed the receiving end of a birth, but I had mentioned Bessie's condition to a couple of doctor friends in Duluth. I asked what I should do in the remote possibility I became involved, and they gave me some suggestions. With this scanty knowledge, I took a boat and motor and followed Abie to their home.

Their house on the Canadian side of the lake was a wooden structure protected from the north winds of winter and facing south to absorb the sun's rays. The front stoop led into a dining room-sitting area which extended by one door to the kitchen and another to a bedroom. I found Bessie in the bedroom well advanced in labor. Abie's mother, an elderly full-blooded Cree Indian who spoke no English, sat near the head of the bed. A triangular "birthing

Bessie Cook and Mrs. John Clark in Front of the Cooks' Home

board" was at the foot of the bed to give traction for Bessie's pushing. Abie and his mother were silent, awaiting my instructions. This was not true of Bessie who was feeling pains at increasing intervals.

I sent Abie to heat water and gave him scissors and string to boil. At least that seemed the logical way to begin. Soon the actual birth started; the top of the head appeared. Then the head was followed by the shoulders. The umbilical cord stayed where it belonged, and all looked normal. The rest of the baby slid out with ease. I turned her over and gave her a swat. She let out a little cry. (I couldn't remember if I was supposed to do that before or after I cut the umbilical cord.) Nature does have a wonderful way of arranging things, for there was one obvious place to make the cut. Abie brought the boiling supplies, and I tied the cord on both sides of the juncture. With some trepidation I severed the connection and placed the baby girl into the waiting arms of her grandmother. The discharge of the afterbirth was a slow delayed process accompanied by some loss of blood. Abie and I changed the bedclothes so when I left Bessie would be neat and clean. I suggested to Abie that he soak the sheets overnight so the blood stains could be removed more easily. The next day I glanced across the lake and saw one person in a boat going back and forth along the shore. It was Abie. He had tied the sheets one behind the other and was towing them behind the motor. This proved to be an effective cleaning method.

I received a large decorated parchment from my medical friends. The words were embellished with sweeping flourishes:

— MIDWIFE —

In God She Trusted

The Rice Harvest

Autumn's tang was in the air. The Indians from Saganaga and Gunflint were making their annual trip to the wild rice fields. They traveled 30 miles east to Whitefish Lake, Ontario, where they would be joined by Indians from

Grand Portage and the Shebandowan Reservation near Lake Lac des Mille Lac. Wild rice was a winter staple, and the time of gathering was a great social event: marriages, news and happenings of the past year were shared by all.

The Plummer family invited me to join them one year, and I observed not only the camaraderie of the event, but the participation of all the family members with different tasks. Each family had their own parching tubs and fires. Each family built and lined their own pits for threshing, and each had their own birchbark baskets for winnowing.

Wild rice grows in muddy shallow lakes where the seasons bring little change in the water level. The stalks of wild rice are like those of wheat, with their grain ripening and swelling out thick and full. The Indians pull their way through the rice beds, two to a canoe.

Walter, who paddled from the bow, lifted his paddle carefully to avoid jarring the ripened rice. His sister, Butchie, sat in the stern with two sticks like batons. She used one to bend the stalks of rice over the side of the canoe and gave a light tap to the heads with the other. The ripe rice fell into the canoe. Immature rice is left to be harvested later, or it may be eaten by migratory ducks, or it may even just drop into the water, reseeding itself.

The gathering of rice is the easiest part of the harvesting process. The canoeload of rice is brought to shore and spread on large sheets of birch bark which are sewn together with split spruce root. Here the rice is dried in the sun for a few hours, and any stem pieces or foreign particles are removed. Small batches are taken from time to time from the birchbark sheet and placed in a metal washtub that is tipped at a 45-degree angle over a small fire. Netowance Plummer stirred the rice with a short paddle. Her motions were even and rhythmic with the knack of years of experience. The entire body of rice not only revolves but folds

Joe Blackjack Cooking Wild Rice

over so that all particles are equally parched. They gradually turn a golden brown.

A predug pit, about two and a half feet across and knee-deep, is lined with shakes of freshly split cedar. At two sides are upright hand rails. Some of the parched rice is poured into the pit, enough to reach a depth of eight to ten inches. New moose hide moccasins with cloth tops folded and tied around the ankle are made especially for the occasion. Walter, the man of the family, slipped on the moccasins and stepped into the pit. He held onto the upright bars with his hands and moved his feet in a lilting, twisting motion, loosening the husks.

This threshed rice is removed from the pit and divided into smaller amounts, which are placed in shallow birchbark baskets. Next comes the winnowing. The women tie their

27

long sleeves at the wrist and wear bandanas around their necks as protection against the drifting chaff. With quick deft movements they toss the rice lightly into the air, the chaff is wafted out, and the rice falls back into the basket, to be flipped and reflipped time and time again.

Then the rice is put back into the pit for a second threshing. The last traces of chaff are removed by tossing once more in the birchbark baskets. Now the rice is clean, light grey in color and ready to use or store through the winter.

In the evenings, the older folks gathered before a campfire and talked of trapping, the abundance or scarcity of game and the condition of the rice still to be harvested. The younger folks strolled off to renew friendships or perhaps do a little courting.

When sufficient rice is gathered and parched, the festivities and camaraderie end. The birchbark sheets are stored in rolls along with the birchbark baskets, both of which are almost indestructable, for the next year's use.

A few years after I accompanied the Plummers to Whitefish, a commercial firm brought in Indians and trucks from other places to harvest rice. The green rice was loaded on the trucks and hauled to a mechanical parching, sorting and packaging plant. At the same time the Canadian Game and Fish Dept. assigned certain harvesting plots to each Indian and laid down rules. This ended the gathering and socializing of the Indians who had harvested rice here for many years. Our Indians no longer traveled to Whitefish in the fall.

Shortly after the rice harvest, the leaves turn color. The birches, aspen and tamarack, now a deep yellow, provide vivid contrast to the pines' dark green. An occasional dash of red moose maple stands out in relief. The forest floor is sprinkled with the purple aster, white button mushrooms, pine needles and fallen leaves. Suddenly one realizes that the woods have lost the song of the warblers, thrushes, vireos and robins. Great flocks of geese gabble and visit as they fly high overhead, their fluttering V formation shimmering in the afternoon sun like a bit of gossamer in the sky. The loons gather in ever larger numbers on the lakes, and then one day they too are gone.

The first snow arrives, laying down each soft flake on a twig, a blade of grass or a pine bough as gently as the first blush of a maiden. The snow birds move down from the north and flit along the trails in flocks, ever restless. The rutting season of the deer has come, and one may meet a doe on a deer trail, her coat a sleek grey like moss on the trees. She may lightly, gracefully and slowly approach as you stand motionless. She may stop, watch you cautiously, twitch her ears and noiselessly turn and vanish in the forest. Perhaps a buck with widespread antlers will follow with his nose close to the ground, intent on the mission of court-ship. He may stop, and with head held high, challenge your intrusion. But then, seeing no danger, he may hesitantly continue and unerringly follow the tracks of the doe.

The waves in the lakes seethe back and forth, daily growing more leaden. On a cold still night, in one quick move, the lakes are stilled as in death. They become blanket-ed securely with a solid skim of ice which slowly, steadily, grows thicker and more binding. Winter is here.

Winter life in the north is like a world apart. Nature sets down fast and hard rules. Observing them means pleasure; ignoring them can mean trouble. The demands are simple — dry matches, an axe, snowshoes, loose-fitting wool clothing, a parka for a windbreak, mitts and liners, and rubber shoe packs. With these few essentials one is comparatively safe in the woods. There could be trouble without any one of them.

In Court

Pete La Plante, an Indian from Grand Portage, often stopped at the lodge. He was a superb woodsman who traveled without a compass but never became lost. One day he came to the store and wanted groceries but had no money. As was customary then, I held something as security until his furs were sold. This time it was a half-dozen beaver hides which I stowed in my cabin. Once he gave me snowshoes — a huge pair that carried me over all snow conditions with ease.

Around this time a Canadian game warden named John Jacobs passed through often, inspecting traplines in his district. He usually pulled a toboggan loaded with bundles. Sometimes he left his bundles at our place, and I took him to Sea Gull by car to save him the time and portages on the Granite River route. U.S. Customs had learned that John was bringing Hudson Bay blankets through to American customers. We were unaware of it, for he often stopped and played cribbage, staying overnight. His act came under the heading of smuggling, and we were accused of aiding and abetting. Immigration, customs officers and game wardens descended on us and searched every building and cranny. They confiscated not only packages John had left with us, but also our eiderdowns purchased many years before, a Canadian canoe on which we had paid duty, a tanned otter hide with a Canadian stamp given to me by Benny Ambrose and alas, Pete La Plante's beaver hides which I had taken as security on his food purchase. We eventually retrieved all the booty except Pete's hides.

I was in deep trouble over those beaver hides. I had hides in my possession out of season, and I had no trapping license. This was a criminal charge, and I was brought to trial. My lawyer wanted me to plead innocent and relate why I had them. If I followed his advice, I would involve Pete and still be charged with aiding and abetting.

At the back of the room stood two rows of Indians — my neighbors and my friends. The judge called me to the bench, after the state attorney made me look like a hardened criminal, and asked what I had to say in my defense.

I answered, "I had the hides in my possession, your Honor and therefore on that count I am guilty."

He peered down at me and said, "You realize that if you plead guilty, the charge will be on your record if you want to teach at any time in the future."

I said, "I am guilty, your Honor."

He replied, "Your fine will be $300."

I must have paled, for this was during the depression, and he could as well have said $3000, for even $10 would have hurt. After a moment he added that the fine would be suspended during a probation period of one year. The Indians silently filed out of the room.

Illegal Buyers

Beaver, the most important animal trapped, was the main sustenance for the Indians and trappers living in this part of the country. Beaver were quite prevalent in 1927, and the prices were high. Kits sold for $40 and adult beaver $60 to $80 depending on the condition of the pelt. The legal beaver limits were not too well observed, and much illegal trapping was done before and after the season. There were illegal fur buyers who came to buy fur trapped during the winter, usually on the American side because we had road access.

The buyers operated quite openly. One came to the lodge with a vicious dog in his car so no one could approach to make an inspection. He made his deal with the trapper and then arranged to pick up the fur at a designated point in the woods. Usually this location was very convenient for the illegal buyer. Some arrangements were made with buyers flying in by plane and landing on the ice. It was a game of tag as well as hide and seek between game wardens Charlie Ott, Art Allen, Art Johnson, Johnny Blackwell and the trappers and illegal buyers. Although everyone knew the game, it was difficult to catch anyone in the act at these scattered night rendezvous.

One early spring just after the ice left the lakes, Ben Ambrose let it be known among the trappers that he knew of a buyer who was paying exceptionally high prices, and this was the man to sell to. The buyer came to Gunflint and went across the lake to appraise the beaver hides. He made a date to rendezvous with Charlie Cook and George Plummer. A couple of days before the pick-up, Walter Plummer stopped at the shed where I was recanvassing a canoe. After a bit of chit-chat I asked Walter if he were going to sell his hides to this buyer. He said, "No, everybody talks too much — too many people know; it's not safe."

George and Charlie brought their beaver hides to the American side to make the contact. Instead of meeting the buyer they expected, they were surrounded by game wardens. The hides were confiscated, and George and Charlie were taken to Duluth and put in jail. It took a week for a neighbor and us to raise the money and arrange their release. In return they split a lot of wood for us that spring.

Both governments made changes that stopped the illegal buying. The Americans made it illegal to possess hides that were not tagged or stamped by the game warden. The Canadians approached it differently. The Ministry of Wildlife divided the territory among the trappers, giving each a specific trapping ground. The trapper was required to count the live houses in his area and mark them on a map for the Game and Fish Dept. Then the authorities determined how many beaver could be taken from each house. The trappers soon learned they could have a viable beaver business by keeping the beaver population in balance with available food. It proved to be a successful operation.

Otter and mink were also trapped, although when mink farms offered a variety of breeds and colored pelts, the wild mink market dropped.

Timber wolves were very abundant at this time, and bounties were paid on both sides of the border. Often when a wolf made a deer kill, a trapper would bury strychnine in the flesh. When the wolf came back to feed on the carcass, it would be poisoned. But smaller animals and birds too became victims when they fed on the remains. Soon the use of this poison was outlawed.

For a time it was legal to hunt wolves from a plane. A small plane would come in, make a low swoop over a wolf sunning himself in the middle of the lake, and a hunter would lean out from the plane and shoot. After two years the wolves learned to hightail it for the woods as soon as they heard a plane. Eventually hunting wolves from the air became illegal, but the wolves took care of it first.

Christmas at Gunflint

At Christmas Mother invited all the Indian neighbors for a big feast. Word spread among them but there was no indication of how many would appear. On the appointed day, we watched for signs of movement across the lake, a mile away. The snow-draped timbered hills made a backdrop to the white ice of the lake, and we could see one moving tiny speck appear on the far shore and then another. The figures of Abie Cook, Bessie and their youngsters were strung out in a long line and became ever larger. In another 10 minutes Netowance Plummer and Mary Cook would appear, snowshoeing with ease, one behind the other. Their layered skirts swayed with each step as they slowly came closer. Although they spoke no English, when they came in, their broad smiles and twinkling eyes revealed their pleasure. Eddie Burnside and his wife arrived next, carrying their youngster in a tick-a-noggin. Charlie Cook joined the Plummers — Walter, Butchie and George — who came, one following the other.

Parkas, caps and mitts were piled in a corner of the dining room. The Indians carefully swept the snow from their moose hide mukluks to keep them dry. The dining room tables were arranged in a long line so we were all seated as one big family. Our friends sat on chairs along the wall waiting and watching quietly while the feast was brought from the kitchen.

One Christmas Mother prepared a large roast. When it was passed to the two older ladies, they looked at it but took none. When we asked, we were informed, "They no eat cow." It was evident that they had eaten contaminated beef once and become ill. Mother quickly found slices of cold turkey which was agreeable to them.

Following Christmas dinner we cleared the table and

Winter Moccasins

all joined in a game of poker, the one game everyone knew. We played plain stud poker for several hours, shifting the piles of chips back and forth. The Indians laughed and joked. I enjoyed hearing them speak. The Chippewa language flows quietly and smoothly like water gliding over a smooth submerged rock. As they tired, they left one by one as quietly as they arrived.

While visiting during the Christmas dinner, we learned Butchie Plummer had never had a birthday party. She was born the year of the big snow. We estimated her age and set her birthday at March 17th. Mother planned her first birthday party and invited all the neighbors. She notified our guests, who responded with gusto sending some gifts and 50 greeting cards. Mother fixed a luncheon and birthday cake with candles. Walt Yocum who had a cabin a short distance down the lake brought his guitar, played and sang hillbilly songs. Butchie asked me to read the cards to her over and over.

My Bitch Meets a Sled Dog

Many trappers and Indian families along the border had dog teams. It all started for me when Nookie, a husky, introduced himself to Doc, my Norwegian elkhound. Nookie lived across the lake on a peninsula with his master John Clark, a trapper and sometimes fishing guide. John made the trapping trails into the Missing Link / Tuscarora Lake area which

John Clark, Trapper

35

with slight modification have become the present canoe routes. Nookie was a handsome dog of unknown lineage who was trained to pull a toboggan with traps and camping sundries and to walk with his nose between John's knees, stepping in the hole created by the overlap of the snowshoes. He never erred by accidentally stepping on a snowshoe and tripping his companion.

My Norwegian elkhound named Doc was a bitch of impeccable lineage, a college present from a friend. On one clear moonlit night when the beams danced on the water and the shadows of the trees added a fringe to the shoreline, Nookie swam across the lake to have a clandestine affair with Doc. As a result she became an enticing strumpet, who strutted and flaunted her wares, and presented us with a continuous succession of litters. I raised the most promising of her puppies for a dog team, and many unsuspecting lodge guests left with puppies curled in their arms as gifts.

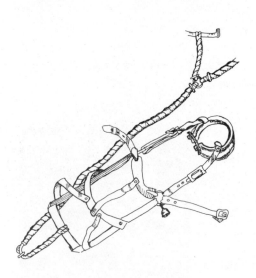

Dog Team Harness

Keeping a dog team entailed many chores. Harnesses, carrying the mixed aroma of dog hair and leather, had to be checked and repaired. Large pails of cornmeal mush had to be cooked daily for the dogs' food. And meat or fish had to be purchased to add nutrient. Cornmeal is filling, but it offers little to contribute to the dogs' endurance or pulling power. To

Wallace Kirkland, Life Magazine © Time Inc.

Driving my Three-Dog Team, 1944

develop stamina, they need meat or fish.

I usually purchased storm herring from Lake Superior fishermen. When that huge lake kicked up its heels, the fishermen were unable to get out to their nets for several days. The catch would be worthless, except for dog food, by the time they could lift their nets.

Every member of a dog team has a different personality. A few dogs are natural-born leaders, others are followers, and some are lazy and may pretend to pull by keeping the traces deceptively taut. Second in importance to the leader is the wheel dog who pulls at a diagonal on a curve to keep the sled or toboggan from sliding off the trail. The remaining

37

dogs are placed according to their aggressiveness. The dogs were driven in a straight line one behind the other. Five to seven dogs usually made up a team, but on occasion three were used for a light load. At Gunflint, having finally trained a team of dogs, I used them for hauling wood, skidding building logs into the construction site and taking winter tourists on short rides. I also drove them on day trips and sometimes on a prolonged trip.

The leader determined the efficiency of the team. I was fortunate when John, one of the pups from my bitch's first litter, became a superb leader. He not only learned the commands (Gee and Haw) but also became adept at feeling out an obliterated trail on a windswept lake. He would help start a heavy load by lunging into his harness which caused the other dogs to do likewise. But there were also times when John became bored with some repetitious task and seemingly forgot all he ever knew.

Although we kept our dogs tied at all times, during the summer we often let one dog loose at a time for exercise. One dog never left the place unless another broke loose — then the two of them were gone. Invariably our loose dogs encountered porcupines, which always presented a challenge to them. Our lead dog John was the only one who learned to leave porcupines alone. After once getting a large quill in his nose and walking up to me to have it removed, he avoided future contacts. When the other dogs found a porcupine, they would threaten it closer and closer. The porcupine would slap its tail quickly, and a dog would be zapped. A porcupine quill has a barb on the end which works in deeper with the victim's muscular movement. If the quill hit a vital organ, the injury could be fatal. Usually the dogs had quills on their faces, inside their mouths and in their chests.

The only effective method I found to remove quills

was stringing the dog's hindquarters to the rafters, but low enough so the shoulders were on the floor, placing a stick through the dog's mouth for it to clamp down on and pulling out the quills one by one with pliers. If the dog's hindquarters weren't lifted off the floor, there was no way of holding him steady.

The only member of our dog team we didn't raise was Egi, a large white Siberian malamute given to us by guests of ours from New Ulm. This couple had traveled in the far north and acquired him as a puppy. In time their lovable ball of fur became a big powerful dog who developed an insatiable desire for their neighbor's chickens — they had to dispose of him. In a last desperate effort to save him, they asked if we might provide him with a home and possibly use him in our dog team. They shipped Egi in a large crate via rail which ended in Two Harbors. I drove the 130 miles to the railhead to pick him up. The men at the express office didn't relish such a large critter in a crate, so I received little help. I reached in, snapped on a chain, broke open the crate and led the dog to the car. As I drove back to Gunflint, he occasionally leaned over from the back seat and licked my ear.

In agreeing to take Egi, there were two things I had not considered. A new and strange dog was not accepted by my other dogs which resulted in many fights, and this dog was not trained for team work. Egi's breaking in period became a struggle of wills. He backed up when the rest of the dogs pulled. He lay down and was dragged on his back with four feet flailing in the air. He stepped out of line on the wrong side of a tree and was slammed into it with a resounding whack. He rushed off the trail and, because of his strength, pulled half the team with him. Each time I reprimanded him, he licked my hand.

Finally in desperation I left him home when I made

the next trip. We kept the dogs tethered on long individual chains, and when I picked up the harnesses there was a complete bedlam. All the dogs wanted a release, a chance to run in the snow and raise their noses to ferret out the scent of a wolf, fox or otter. Although a dog team trip is a disciplined run for the dogs, a comradeship develops between driver and dogs. Egi, excluded, howled and moaned. His banishment lasted three days. Like a child who bundles his most cherished belongings in a bandana tied to a stick and trudges off to conquer the world but finds it frightening and comes back home for supper, so Egi apparently had contemplated his fate. I tried him once more in the team. He submitted to training and became a valuable asset.

Raising dogs and running a resort sometimes created opposing problems. In the summer the dogs were not worked and chafed for a run. Guests invariably wandered among them so it was paramount we not have a vicious dog in our string. It was essential they stay quiet at night and not disturb the guests, but when a bear came near, they created an uproar. One morning at daylight I made three trips to the kennels to quiet the dogs only to discover their howling was instigated by a guest, Dr. Gould. He had been a member of an Antarctic expedition the year before and he was nostalgic for the howl of a bunch of tethered sled dogs. Each time he emitted a wailing call, the entire chorus answered.

Butchie's Trapline

With the arrival of winter the snowshoe rabbit and weasel acquire their protective coats of white. The woods become silent except for the ever present call of the chickadee, the resounding thump of the woodpecker on a succulent tree, the tiny nuthatch's "yank, yank" and the whiskey jack's innumerable murmurs as it glides quietly to pick up a stray morsel of food. The beavers have long since stored their food, interlacing limbs of aspen under the ice in front of their houses. Their "at home" existence is noted by a little of the brush protruding through the ice and a frost-covered vent hole in the center of their dome shaped shelter.

In the late fall and early winter the Indians concentrated on beaver trapping. Butchie always trapped with her mother, but one year Netowance was not able to make the trip and Butchie asked me to go with her. Being a non-resident in Canada, I was allowed only to accompany and assist her.

My previous trapping experience had been for mink with haphazard results. Mink traps are usually set underwater at the entrance to a small manmade rock hut. A fish head for bait is impaled on a stick which is secured in the ground at the back of the structure. The trap is set so when the mink steps into the trap, it makes a jump for freedom, landing in deeper water and drowns with the weight of the trap. If the trap catches only a paw, the mink may chew it off and swim away minus a "hand" or foot.

During my trapping efforts I once caught a mink by the front paw. As I looked at my defiant mink, guilt swept over me for causing such pain. (A real trapper cannot dwell on such sentiments.) I grabbed the mink at the back of the neck with my gloved hands, released it from the trap and housed it in a cabin vacant for the winter to recover from its injury.

Each day I brought a piece of meat which it would consume after I left. After several days I discovered the mink had made a deep and elongated hole in the mattress and established this as its home. Mother was quite upset!

I spent hours trying to get this mink to feed from my

hand, but a mutual fear existed. The mink hid in the farthest corner under the bed while I lay on my belly on the floor reaching toward it with a chunk of meat. It stretched its neck as far as it deemed feasible. It crept forward with a few cautious steps. Suddenly it let out a piercing scream, thumped its feet and backed into a corner. The unexpected sound and movement inevitably sent me recoiling with, I presume, the fear of a bite.

One day I brought in a partridge carcass which it promptly hauled into a partially opened dresser drawer. The mink spent part of its time in the warmth and comfort of the feathers. When I approached, it would hang over the back of the drawer to watch me, leaving its tail and rear end exposed to attack. My touch would send it to a corner, sometimes accompanied by that loud screech and thump of the feet.

I kept the mink until the season had long since closed and traps were lifted. When the creeks and rivulets shook their winter mantle, I left the cabin door ajar so the mink could "escape" and roam free again.

It was with these trapping credentials that I joined Butchie on her trapline on a December day.

We snowshoed the two and one-half mile winter portage overland from Magnetic Bay to Granite Lake, where Butchie had a trapping cabin. Travel was easy for the trail was kept well-packed and hard with use. There were places where moose had discovered this cleared winter pathway and left a frail lacy route intricately designed by the deep imprint of their hooves.

Most winter trails bypass rapids, falls or precarious travel conditions. They go through level frozen swamps which are amply sprinkled with black spruce and tamarack. In summer these trails are sodden underfoot, but thick moss, ferns and an abundance of flowers transform them into a colorful carpet but a haven for blackflies.

In our packsacks we carried only our personal needs — extra socks, underwear and a toothbrush because all other necessary items were in the cabin. The traps were "cached" near the sites where they would be used.

Once at the cabin we established ourselves. The building, about 8x10, was constructed of unpeeled pine logs. Two built-in bunks, head to head, occupied one corner. They were made of poles and piled with balsam boughs, some of which were freshened and replaced with each use. Next to the table was a small airtight stove which served for both heating and cooking. There was a single window reinforced on the outside with old crosscut saw blades to discourage marauding bears. Beside the table was a metal garbage can filled with the staples: flour, sugar, salt, baking powder and dried fruits — all the necessary ingredients for bannock. A kerosene lamp sat on the table and pegs for hanging clothes and mitts to dry were located around the limited wall space.

On the lake a stick protruded through the ice, marking the spot where canned goods confined in a gunny sack were submerged to prevent freezing. We chiseled a hole over the cache, pulled up the sack and found an ample supply of canned beans, vegetables and fruits. Then we walked out a short distance from shore to cut a water hole through two feet of ice. With the last strike the water came bubbling to the surface. We hauled two pails of water to the cabin, marked the hole with a stick and covered it with snow to deter a quick refreeze.

When Butchie caught a beaver, we would have fresh meat, as the saddle and liver of this animal are particularly tasty. A number of trappers prefer the meat of the beaver tail, but it is too fatty for my palate.

We would return each evening to this cabin — our

Butchie with her Beaver Catch

headquarters — after tending a series of traplines arranged in a huge circle.

Carrying an axe and chisel, we started out each morning snowshoeing near creeks and small ponds where the wildlife appeared to be concentrated. The beaver traps, cached at strategic places each year, were retrieved where needed. At each live beaver house Butchie fastened a fresh piece of poplar and a trap to a sturdy but dead pole. She slipped this set under the ice near the beaver's runway. It would be checked every other day.

As we started through a spruce and jack pine forest, Butchie pointed out a platform her mother had built to keep freshly killed moose meat safe from the wolves. We passed through a cluster of spruce laden with snow. Butchie was a short distance ahead of me, and as I called to her, my voice was muted circling within the snow covered trees which effectively acted as a barrier. Along one stream she

44

was preparing a trap while I was chiseling another hole. The stream had several open pockets where the water gurgled over rocks. Suddenly, a beaver appeared through a hole to see what all the disturbance was about. Butchie called, "Hit him, get him." I was amused by this inquisitive beaver, which slowly sank out of sight. Butchie never did get a beaver from this set, but she did reap a harvest from other scattered houses.

Butchie rough-skinned the beaver when they were caught, and we took the choice cuts of meat for food. Back at camp Butchie fleshed the hides of all fat. Then she rolled them to keep them frozen until we returned home. There Butchie could leisurely thaw the hides, then stretch them and lace them to ash hoops for drying. When they were removed from the hoops, they were ready to be shipped to a clearing house and the fur sales. Then Butchie was assured money for food for the winter.

A Dog Team Trip

In 1931 I invited Gene Bayle to join me on a weeklong dog team trip to visit Art Smith at his trapping and hunting cabin on Mountain Lake. We packed the toboggan carefully with sleeping bags, food for ourselves and the dogs and the necessary cooking pails. The dog team toboggans were long, narrow and limber, which enabled them to fit a snowshoe trail and snake over uneven ground. We started with a speedy dash, but the dogs soon settled into a steady trot. As we approached Charlie Olson's cabin down Gunflint a little way, we saw him on the lake getting a pail of water. Although we had barely started, he insisted we stop for a cup of coffee.

Charlie was active in spite of his 75 years. He skied up to our lodge at least once a week, cut his own wood, did

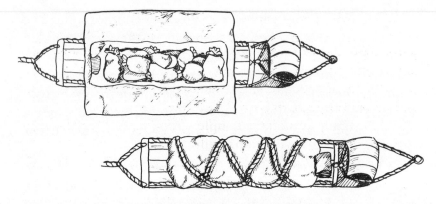

Packing a Dog Team Toboggan

his own cooking, washing and chores. He lived alone with his dog. He was born in Norway, in a region that looks very much like the Gunflint area, and he retained his Norwegian accent. For years he was a logger in the northwoods camps. Many fellows like Charlie are rugged, gruff and painfully outspoken, but under their hard exteriors they are kind and generous. They remind me of an old Indian legend which says that no man can live among the pines who is not at peace with himself.

We stepped into Charlie's spotless cabin. The floor looked freshly scrubbed and the bed was neatly made. Charlie motioned us to sit at his table where he offered butter, crackers, maple syrup and strong black coffee.

"You have a lot of birds feeding on your bird shelf, Charlie."

"Oh, yah! Two pair nuthatches, six pair chickadees, two pair small voodpeckers, und four pair large uns. De viskey yaks steal so much. Ay chase dem away. De nuthatches coom to me every year. De voodpeckers eat such a lot, soon I'll have to buy more suet."

"What shape are the deer in, Charlie?"

"Oh de deer are awful poor. Ay've been cuttin cedar

for dem every day. De game vardens promised me hay but ay ain't got any yet. Last night five deer coom down in de yard. Split Ear is back again dis year. Ay seen him yust last night ven ay was cuttin wood."

"What are you going to make with the diamond willow and cedar you have drying?" we asked.

"At tank ay make a couple of chairs wit de cedar and a sideboard wit de diamond villow. Oh it's a lot of vor-rk. Ay had a hard time finding de diamond villow last fall. Looked all over to get some goot pieces. Vere ya goin?"

We answered, "Down to Mountain Lake, going to be gone almost a week."

"Yah! Vell yore dogs look in good shape — dat team dat vas here yesterday vas so poor ya cud see tru em like paper. Vell ya haf a long vay, ya better get goin."

We pulled on our parkas, hopped onto the toboggan and started down the lake — the dogs traveling fast. The sun transformed everything into a dazzling whiteness. The only shadows were those of the dogs, bouncing along easily on the glistening blue-white snow, followed by two shapeless and practically motionless forms — Gene and me on the toboggan.

Far down the lake we saw a dark object on the ice that appeared to be a stump. As we approached, it took the form of a fox sitting on its haunches. Because we were up wind, the fox wasn't startled. We came within fifty feet of him, then the fox started to lope lazily in a half circle. The dogs wheeled fast at full speed. Suddenly the fox got a whiff of us and became a receding streak, zigzagging across the ice. In a moment he was all of two miles up the lake, then he disappeared behind a point and was gone.

In a short time we reached the inlet where Little Gunflint flows into Gunflint Lake. The current here can make the ice unsafe, so we followed the old railroad spur on land for a short way. About halfway over this portage we stopped to cook up. We unpacked our tea pail, in which we had a little tea, sugar, cups and a couple of sandwiches. While Gene went down to the mouth of Little Gunflint for water, I kicked around for some dry poplar, often called squaw wood, which makes a quick hot fire.

I cut a green tag alder, trimmed the branches, stuck the heavy end in the snow and angled it to hold the tea pail. I gathered a handful of birch bark and had the fire going when Gene returned. We hung the pail on the tag alder over the fire and went back into the woods to gather balsam boughs to sit on.

While gazing pensively into the fire and waiting for the water to boil, we remembered a poem by Bliss Carman in *Songs from Vagabondia:*

> "Here we are free / To be good or bad,
> Sane or mad, / Merry or grim
> As the mood may be, — / Free as the whim
> Of a spook on a spree —"

As we ate our lunch, the dogs eyed us with drooling anticipation, watching each bite disappear. We kicked snow on the fire and resumed our journey.

The dogs started out with renewed vigor after their brief rest. As we jogged past the rapids, the trees squeaked with their coatings of ice formed from the open water's steam in winter air. Delicate fingers of ice, more beautiful than etched crystal, extended from the shore above the rushing water. The snow on the rocks appeared to be covered with a pure white fuzz. On closer examination we saw tiny clusters of ice perfectly shaped and as exact in design as snowflakes.

As we pulled out onto the lake ice, again we saw a dark object on the ice ahead of us. It looked like an old blanket which had been tossed aside. As we came closer we recognized the hide of a deer — skinned as neatly as if done with a knife — and a few bones, surrounded by wolf tracks.

We drove out onto North Lake, a six-mile white expanse bordered by high dark hills. This lake, like most in the area, lies east and west with the higher more abrupt

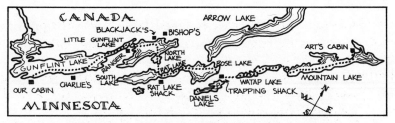

Route of our Dog Team Trip to Mountain Lake

cliffs on the south side and gentler slopes on the north. We skirted the lake on the northern shore, taking turns trotting after the toboggan to keep warm.

Joe Blackjack's cabin was located halfway down the lake. He spoke very little English but he worked for me for several years with the willingness and strength of an ox. I have watched him shoulder a log eight feet long and walk off with ease. His wife once gave me a woven rug made from strips of the inner bark of cedar trees, colored with dyes made from boiling woody plants.

Joe lived with his wife, children and innumerable dogs. This Indian family, different from our closer neighbors, lived in the crudest manner without much cleanliness. When we approached their cabin, a chorus of howls greeted us from a motley pack of nondescript dogs. The door opened and Joe came out to greet us. Behind him, framed in the doorway, four curious children were peering out. Joe, dark, swarthy, stockily built and very bowlegged was a full-blooded Chippewa. His open shirt revealed a bare chest. His unkept hair and the general appearance of his face and hands answered any doubts about his personal hygiene. His children substantiated the same thought.

Judging by the appearance of the walls and roof, their cabin barely hung together with the family dependent on their own huddled numbers for warmth in cold weather. There were no windows to give light, and a dirt floor was within. To Joe, his wife and six children, it was home.

49

A couple of Joe's well-placed kicks cleared the dogs to one side as he came down to meet us with a big grin of welcome.

"Bi-jou."

"Bi-jou, Joe. How's everything?"

A happy grin and a shrug of his shoulders were followed by, "Trapping no good." That told us that he and his family were well but that he, as usual, was broke and about out of chuck.

"Got snuff?"

"Sure, Joe," I said, and handed him two boxes which I had brought for him. He opened one box at once and helped himself to a generous amount. Then he turned and tossed the other box toward the doorway. One scramble and the children had opened the box and partaken of its contents.

"Where you go?"

"Mountain Lake, Joe."

A cheerful grunt, then a wave of his hand was our parting signal. We headed for Sac Bay where there was a hard trail following an old logging road to the Rat Lake

Trappers Cabin at Daniels Lake

portage. The spruce and balsam, so heavy with snow, almost
arched the trail in a white and green bower. Here we were
protected from the wind and had a feeling of snug warmth.
Where the white draped branches of a tall pine ended, a
snow covered balsam took over producing a feather-bed
slope down to the ground.

After the portage we came to Rat Lake — not much
more than a beaver pond separated from Mud Bay by a
narrow spit of land. On this bit of land was an old trapping
shack which Art Smith used occasionally, so we decided
to stop and look inside. Art had told me once that he
usually left a little chuck under an old trap door in the
floor. There was a tiny airtight stove, a pole bed covered
with balsam boughs, a table, a couple of fox stretchers,
several mink stretchers and in the far corner was a homemade mouse trap. A bit of kindling and chips were piled
beside the stove. I spied the trap door and pulled it open.
There in a shallow pit were three cans of beans.

Next we drove down Mud Bay and on to Rose Lake.
High cliffs towered above us on our right. Bits of moss
topped with snow clung in tiny crevasses to the otherwise
bare cliff face.

A little beyond was "stairway portage" to Duncan
Lake — a series of log steps imbedded in the earth. A small
stream tumbled down the cliff in a series of little falls on
one side of the portage. On the opposite side more cliffs
guarded the entrance to Arrow Lake. An old Indian legend
says the Indians competed here in shooting arrows to the
top. We continued to an abandoned railroad bed and then
turned onto a steady incline for about a mile to Daniels
Lake where there was another trapper's cabin.

We arrived just as the sun was dipping behind the hills,
and the evening chill was descending. We unhitched the
dogs, tied them to trees and gathered some balsam boughs

for their beds. Then we unroped the canvas covering our gear and moved in. In the sky to the west color streamers were flying. The setting of the sun was followed by long black banners unfurled by the wind, then the shadows blended and night came.

This cabin had two double bunks of fresh balsam, a small airtight in one corner and a table by the window with two stumps for stools. In a short time we had a fire going. We threw our eiderdowns on our bunks and started supper. I mixed a little bannock dough consisting of flour, baking powder, salt and canned milk. Bannock resembles baking powder biscuits and is a good substitute for bread. The dough is flattened out and fried until it raises and turns brown. Then it is flipped and topped with brown sugar.

After supper, with the dogs fed and dishes washed, we sat at the table. By flickering candlelight we looked over an old magazine we flushed from a corner of the cabin. I tossed an extra chunk of wood into the airtight and it began to sing. The wood was alive again, once more standing tall in the forest, its sap running up to its branches and the soft south winds creeping through the leaves. Like a record playing for the last time, the wood told of life among its fellows. Then it crumbled to ashes — source of nourishment for another tree.

We blew out the candle and climbed into our eiderdowns. The warmth of the bags, the scent of the balsam boughs, the long squeak of two trees as they rubbed together outside the cabin and the tiny rustle and gnawing of wood borers working under the bark on the cabin logs all added to our contentment. A light from a crack in the lid of the airtight flickered on the ceiling, and soon even this disappeared.

The next morning was considerably warmer with a bright sun. By this time Gene and I had evolved a natural sharing of work. Gene set the table and got fresh water while I cooked breakfast. She did the dishes while I replenished the wood supply and repacked the toboggan. We hitched the dogs, took a last look and were ready for our trip to Mountain Lake. We followed Art's trapping trail, crossing a little stream which was the boundary between the United States and Canada. Tracks indicated a mink had followed this route in search of food.

This old trail from Daniels Lake to Watap Lake has been traveled by hundreds of couriers and Indians packing out fur in the spring. It has felt the soft pads of innumerable dog teams. The trail follows a draw, well protected by hills, where the sun only penetrates in small patches. We entered a tag alder swamp just before reaching Watap Lake. As we came onto the lake we stopped and made birchbark goggles with just a slit in front, to eliminate glare from the snow and prevent snow blindness.

The morning was balmy with a sniff of spring in the air. As the toboggan slipped along, we threw back our parka hoods and pulled the liners out of our mitts. As the sun rose higher, we shed our parkas and pulled out one set of shirttails. (We wore two wool shirts one over the other.)

Halfway down the lake we noticed a live beaver house along the shore. Beaver have their front door underwater but they live in their house above the water line. In front of the house the ice is always thin from their underwater travels. Anyone trespassing too closely is assured an icy bath. In winter beaver trappers make their sets under the ice. A good trapper will take only a few beaver from each house, preventing the depletion of his own trapping grounds. In spring one can hear the little beavers a'talking in the house.

It was a short run to the portage, up the hill — down the other side and out onto Mountain Lake. The lake stretched ahead for six miles, guarded on both sides by high hills. The heavily wooded hills slipped by, dark in their wild secrets — a woods dense and at times uncompromising. We could hear the soft rustle of the snow as it whooshed off the fir trees. The branches, released from their weight, bobbed up and down as if trying to restore their circulation. We rounded the last bend and saw fresh smoke puffing from the cabin chimney.

As we approached the cabin Art opened the door, leaned against the door jamb and asked,

"How's the going?"

"Good," we answered, "we came right along."

"I seen Harry when he came through so I knowed you would be along. Tie your dogs out to those trees and I'll yank the toboggan in the cabin and unload."

The cabin was littered with wood chips. Art was in the process of making a runner for a new sled and drying slabs of cedar to be shaped into paddles. In one corner were some burls from birch which he would make into bowls and cups and saucers. Some fellows have the knack of making about anything out of wood, and Art was

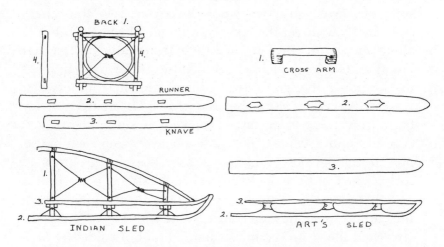

Art's Sled Compared to an Indian Sled

one of them. Even the wooden door hinges he had made were functional. He remarked, "I've been working on this sled; the parts are about finished. All I need are a few bolts to hold the parts together. This sled will be light and good for traveling in the spring. I fixed it for you, you can take the parts back, get some bolts and sometime when I'm up that way I'll help you put it together."

"How's trapping, Art?" we asked.

"There's not much. No goddam game left in the country. It ain't worthwhile for all the running around you have to do. The country is about ruined, too many people. Fishing ain't much good anymore, no marten left, hardly any fisher or otter, only a few mink and weasels and every time you look for a beaver the goddam game wardens are snooping around. There ain't any game left in the country at all. When the logging camp was here, I was hired to shoot moose for the camp, and that was easy. You couldn't do that now; even the moose have moved out. There ain't no caribou, and there used to be some of those up here. There ain't enough game in the goddam country to make a good living from anymore. Think I'll go further north where there is still some fur."

It was late so we busied ourselves getting dinner. Art stepped to the door, reached up on the roof where he had cached a moose heart for dinner. He cooked the meal while we went to the lake to the water hole. This one was covered with a bottomless box, well packed on the sides with snow, with a lid to deter a fast freeze. By the time we were back and carried in a few armfuls of wood, Art had the meal on the table. After cooking for the dogs and washing the dishes, we watched the long afternoon shadows retreat step by step and vanish on the far side of the lake.

Art said, "I've got a trap down here about a mile; ain't seen it for a couple of days. Want to put on your snowshoes and come along?"

"We're with you," we answered. We hiked down the lake to a live beaver house. Art chopped a hole in the ice, pulled out the trap with a beaver in it and tossed both of them in his pack. He was taking no more beaver from this house for this year.

We returned to the cabin and watched while Art skinned the beaver. Deftly he slit the belly from the tail to the tip of the nose. He made four circular cuts, one at each wrist so later the feet could be pulled through the apertures, and then skinned the animal in just a few minutes. The hide was clean, golden in color, and showed no evidence of grease which if left could cause a "burn" when the hide dried.

He picked up a hoop he had made by bending, twisting and then tying a couple of young ash sticks together. He threaded a large curved hide needle with light meter line and sewed the hide into the hoop. He stretched and sewed at the same time, creating a "blanket," which was slightly oblong but had well-rounded sides. After he completed the work to his satisfaction, he put the hide in a cool corner of the cabin. In three or four days the hide would be dry. Then the fur could be brushed and the hide rolled into a loose bundle for packing out later.

The next morning continued warm and we busied ourselves, under Art's guidance, making wire snares for rabbits. Gene took four and I took four, and we headed for the nearby patch of green timber where there were a number of trails. We picked places where the rabbits traveled under windfalls. We shoved down sticks on each side of their trail leaving just enough room for them to travel through. Then we hung our snare in the center of the runway a couple of inches off the ground. It took us some time to find the best spots and to arrange everything just right. We looked back, as we returned to the cabin, in anticipation of a rabbit stew.

Gene and Art began whittling small paddles from pieces of dry cedar, while I busied myself making first a holster for my .22 Woodsman Colt from an old piece of leather boot and then a knife

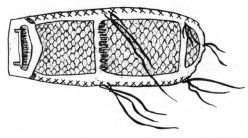

Knife Sheath made from a Beaver Tail

sheath from a beaver tail. We were an industrious group.

Suddenly Gene stopped whittling and said, "You know a vacation in the bush can put a person's feet back on solid earth, renew perspective and give one a dioramic outlook on life when the surface has become flat without light or shadow."

"H-u-m-m-ph," Art grunted, "The city is no place to live. Just a jammed-up bunch of people, one living on top of the other. They talk so much about lakes that they have fixed up. Why hell, they ain't as big as one of these damned old beaver ponds. They ain't got no fish, except for a few about as big as yore finger — then they go out and set all day to catch those. No game except what they have tied up in their parks or stuffed in their museums. Oh I've been down there — everyone running around in such a hurry, cars banging up and down the street, people milling in and out of the stores. Why I bet half of them don't know where they're going or why they're in such a big hurry. Then look at all the smoke and dirt hanging over one of those places — you can hardly breathe, let alone see the sun — people setting in offices all day with lights on — hell, that ain't livin' — it ain't even hardly existin'. Nope, this is the kind of country to live in, only there ought to be more game so a man could make a good living without having to run all over the country for one lousy mink or weasel."

57

Art's paddle was swiftly taking shape when he said, "There ain't much good cedar around. You look until you find a tree where the bark markings are straight up and down. Most of them go around the trunk and they aren't straight-grained. You have to cut the length you want and then bring it in to dry. You dassn't use the center because the core ain't no good but you use a slab, free of knots, alongside the core. Sometimes you can find a dry cedar that the Indians have stripped aways to make bark baskets. You can tell them by the checks in the tree. Lots of times in trees you find like this wood has lost its life. It is usually good enough for making ribs for a canoe."

In midafternoon we decided to check our snares to see if we had a rabbit for supper. As we stepped out of the cabin the sun was sliding down over the hill. Gene and I were both a bit disappointed to find our snares untouched. We cooked up and after eating climbed onto our bunks, comfortable and content. We planned to start home the next day. Art would go with us as far as the Daniels Lake shack where he would turn off and go to Clearwater to get more food.

Suddenly out of the darkness came a shriek like the shrill cry of a child. We dashed out to our snares. Sure enough there was a rabbit. In our chagrin for causing such pain we quickly took him out of the snare, but he just lay there on the snow in the clear moonlight mortally hurt, gazing at us with his big soft eyes. We felt sick in spirit and didn't much want to have the fellow for a stew. Art looked at us with an understanding smile. While we picked up the rest of our snares, Art cleaned the rabbit and set it on a rafter for a meal upon his return.

The following morning there was a slight snow flurry. We spent a couple of hours around camp, packing up and gathering a good stockpile of wood for the cabin. The snow was coming down a little faster by the time we were ready to start. Art snowshoed ahead, and as we drove out of the bay and around the point, the fury of the storm struck us head-on. Art stopped and said, "It looks as if it might be tough."

We proceeded down the lake, and the storm became a seething, swirling mass of snow. It was like a thick fog obliterating all the shorelines and leaving us with no sense of direction. John, the lead dog, stopped and looked back. We got off the toboggan and put on our snowshoes. I went ahead to break trail while Gene followed the dogs. It was almost impossible for me to follow Art's windswept track although he was only a few yards ahead.

It was, as Art had predicted, tough going. The hoar frost from our breath froze on our chins and the fur of our parka hoods. Snow gathered on our eyebrows and eyelashes. The dogs' faces were encased in white. Just dangling tongues and sets of eyes indicated they were dogs. I turned to see if Gene were following. With my back to the wind I thought how easy it would be to travel with the storm like coasting downhill. As we pushed on, our pace slowed. The toboggan was dragging hard and the dogs had begun to tire. We moved like robots leaning into the blizzard. At times the snow swirled deep into our noses and throats almost restricting our air supply. For a second the storm lifted, and I saw Art standing far ahead of us and over on the shoreline. We headed in that direction, but all was blotted out again. In fifteen minutes or a half hour or maybe more, we pulled into a tiny sheltered bay. Here there was no wind, just a fine sifting snow coming down through the trees.

Art looked us over carefully and then said casually, "We're about halfway. I believe we'd better pull into the swamp here and camp for the night. It's almost three o'clock and we can't make it in against this storm before dark."

The cedar swamp was well protected, and soon we had a fire going. It was a relief to get out of that driving snow.

"I'll fix a lean-to over here and the two of you get a big bunch of balsam boughs," Art said as he shoveled snow with his snowshoe. He built a shelter and carefully placed the boughs we had gathered on top like a thatched roof. We piled a thick layer of boughs on the ground inside the shelter and had our house completed. Art dragged in enough wood to last through the night while we bedded the dogs, unpacked and melted snow for coffee and cooking. After supper we sat inside our shelter on our two eiderdowns enjoying the warmth of the fire and protection from the snow. At Art's suggestion we clipped the two eiderdowns together, removed our parkas, outer shirts and moccasins and all slipped into the enlarged sleeping bag. From far off we heard one long mournful howl of a timber wolf. Egi, the malamute, lifted his snoot to the sky and answered. We slept the deep sleep of the weary.

Sometime in the night or early morning I became acutely aware that the storm had abated, the fire was out, and it had turned very cold. From then on we slept restlessly, not cold and yet not warm — just on the margin of comfortably uncomfortable. By daylight the trees were snapping with the cold, the top edge of the eiderdowns was covered with hoar frost from our breath, and the dogs were curled into tiny white

*Balsam Lean-to Constructed
for a Storm Shelter*

humps. We drew lots as to who would get out to start the fire and cook breakfast. I pulled the unlucky draw, and as I crawled out into the numbing cold, I wasn't particularly pleased with the smug looks of satisfaction on my companions' faces.

Breakfast was corn fritters and coffee. The snow squeaked underfoot as it does in intense cold. The fritters almost cooled while cooking, which led me to believe it was colder than forty below zero. By the time they landed on our plates, all warmth had completely departed. The coffee, however, did stay hot until it could be downed. We did not tarry long after this meal, as we felt we had to keep moving to keep warm.

In a surprisingly short time we had packed, hitched the dogs and were ready to leave our comfortable quarters. We had Nookie on lead because he was trained to follow a breaking trail and never stepped on the tail of a snowshoe. John was moved back into the team; he dropped his tail, flopped his ears and sulked. He still pulled, but only like one who was highly bored with a most unpleasant task.

Soon we were at the parting of our ways. Art went on to Clearwater while we turned back to Rose Lake and our return home. We took turns, riding and trotting, and about noon we stopped at the North-South Lake portage to cook lunch. Just as the tea water was boiling, George Plummer came around the point. He knew a shortcut to Gunflint and offered to show us the way. We traveled up an arm of North Lake, into a cedar swamp through which a very crooked trail had been cut, continued across a beaver pond, through more cedar swamp and out onto Gunflint. Mile after mile Georgie trotted beside us with no hesitation — a tribute to a good physique. We were opposite Charlie Olson's cabin as the curtain of darkness descended. The night was clear, crisp and blue. Some of the brilliance seemed to come from below, crystals of snow winking back the starlight. The lake groaned and moaned as its bars of ice were strengthened. A person alone on such a cold night is glad for the friendly squeak of snowshoes on cold snow. But the two of us riding behind the dogs toward a familiar glow of light reveled in the feeling of belonging to a world apart.

An epoch of time passes — an historical interim — for trappers of this breed are no longer. These men of the woods would guide canoe parties in the summer but seldom a fishing party — only if they were fly fishermen. This handful of local men, Art Smith of North Lake - Gunflint - Clearwater or wherever he hung his hat; Jimmy Dunn of Sea Gull; Jack Dewar from Loon Lake; John Clark at Gunflint; Benny Ambrose of Otter Track Lake, gave to any party they took on a trip an unforgettable experience and a feeling of comfort in the woods. People from all over were privileged to travel with these experienced and congenial men. They were replaced by college boys who became known as fishing guides.

Resort Expansion

When Mother bought this fishing camp, she wanted a first-class resort. She hired a local contractor in Grand Marais to build two new cabins, a boat house and an addition on each end of the existing lodge building. The south addition was to be the dining room and the north addition a lounge. George Bayle, Gene's father, was hired to build native furnishings for the two rooms. A large fireplace was added to each room. The old portion of the lodge became our office and the store for our Indian neighbors, since they had no direct access to a food supply.

The Expanded Lodge Building, 1928

The following year, in 1929, Mother purchased an island on Saganaga Lake from a man in Duluth. The Trail was extended to Sea Gull in 1930. Mother hired George Bayle and his brother Joe to build a small lodge and one cabin on the island to serve as an outpost for Gunflint Lodge. Sleeping accommodations were in tents on platforms. This new enterprise was called Saganaga Lodge.

Bunkhouse at the Tent Camp on Saganaga

63

CHAPTER 3

"THE ECONOMY GOES BUST"

Learning to Guide

GENE Bayle, my friend from Grand Marais, taught me the proper way to handle a canoe. After a week of practice, up and down rapids and in the wind, I became comfortable as a stern paddler. This new art served me well, for in the struggle to pay our bills, I worked into a guiding routine of paddling a canoeload of guests the 16 miles (including four rapids and eight portages) to Saganaga Lodge and picking up a return group to go back the six miles to Gunflint Lodge via two rapids, a portage and across Sea Gull Lake where we were met by the lodge truck.

Gene Bayle and Val McIlhenney (a classmate from college) operated Saganaga Lodge located on our island in Saganaga Lake. We packed all food and equipment over the Sea Gull-Saganaga portage, canoed it down Sea Gull River and the two small rapids to Saganaga Lake. From that point it was a six-mile run with a small motor up Saganaga Lake to our island. Most of the guests for this outpost came from Gunflint by canoe, down the Granite River, with an overnight or sometimes a week stay at our island lodge.

At times, as I heaved a heavy canvas-covered canoe onto my shoulders at a portage making this round trip, I thought, "There must be an easier way than this to make a living."

64

Money is spent and forgotten, while unforgettable memories linger on. I recall one night in particular. I took a canoeload of people down the Granite River to our island, where they would stay for several days. I picked up three other guests for a return to Gunflint. Reflected beams from the full moon danced on the water beside us as we glided silently between the islands. An array of northern lights undulated their colors back and forth across the sky. They were suddenly replaced by convoluted curtains of color extending down to us from infinity. We had the feeling of being engulfed in this mysterious force. As we watched, this display gradually faded. It was replaced by searchlight beams vying in intensity. Portaging to Sea Gull Lake we severed the tree shadows that crossed our path. The moon's reflected light defined a path to the landing where the truck was waiting for our return to Gunflint.

Many of my days were spent guiding fishing parties on Gunflint Lake. At this time these lakes held only lake trout and northern pike with the former predominant in the deeper lakes. Northern pike prefer weedy shallow bays which are not abundant in Gunflint Lake. The fishing parties were mostly men, but on a few occasions there were couples. Many times day trips went as far as Granite Lake where, although portages were involved, the guests could better appreciate these narrow waterways. Birds, a beaver or otter were sometimes seen and northern pike was easily caught and available for a noon cookup.

It was always a pleasure for me to have my guests enjoy all the facets of this country rather than just fish to catch a limit. I especially liked guiding because I became more closely associated with our clientele. As many guests returned year after year, we developed a camaraderie — one large family who enjoyed this remote area for the unique beauty it had to offer.

65

Earl Zerbach and Me with a Catch, late 1930s

On one rare occasion I took two women on a week canoe trip. We took a route to the southern arm of Knife Lake and planned to take a shortcut, which I had used once before, over a few hills and lakes to Otter Track Lake.

Maps were quite inadequate at this time, and portages were unmarked except for a few faded blazes on scattered trees. I had a compass and a sketchy map I used to check off the landmarks as I paddled. In spite of all the attractions, birds and beaver houses that I pointed out to the two women, their one desire was to see how rapidly they could go from one portage to the next. They kept a diary noting times consumed over each lake and each portage traversed.

We crossed the Eddy Lake portage and turned to paddle east to the end of the Knife Lake bay. When I reached the end of the bay, I suggested the women wait in the canoe while I hunted the blaze marks and found the trail to the next lake. I left my compass and map in the bottom of the canoe since I would be gone only a moment.

I found a path which could be the portage. It seemed familiar and yet a little different from the one I remembered. I went further and came to a large pond which didn't look right either. Thinking the trail was further to my left, I searched in that direction. Then I turned to head back to the canoe. I found myself hopelessly lost in unfamiliar country, on an overcast day, without a compass.

Momentarily I was overcome with utter panic. I felt nauseated as thoughts whizzed through my mind. No compass, no matches, no protection from the elements. Gone for a week so no one would make a search for several days, plus the unpredictable reaction of two novice canoeists for whom I was responsible. It took all my willpower to calm down.

I was in a stand of large jack pine whose limbs obligingly extended to the ground. I climbed to the top of one jack pine and thought I could see a hidden valley between two hills which could contain the waterway where I had left the canoe. I shouted from the top of the tree but there was no answer. A light spot momentarily appeared on the horizon. When I climbed down I blazed the tree on four sides with my knife and marked the initials N, S, E and W.

I used this large jack pine as my anchor point and headed south, which I thought was the right direction. I broke twigs to mark my path, constantly sighting back, first toward the tree and then down my straight line of broken branches. In about an hour I came to the exact jack pine from which I started. I had completed a large perfect circle.

Once more I climbed to the top of the jack pine and with two fingers whistled a shrill whistle. Way off in the distance I heard an answer. Then it was clear that I had become entangled in a series of small ridges. I started toward the whistle and after every two or three ridges I crossed, I climbed another jack pine and whistled. Each time the answer was closer. When I reached the canoe, I discovered the women had not stirred. They sat all those hours visiting. My relief was unbounded.

We paddled out of this bay, went around a point and into the next bay to the north where I found the portage easily. It was over a year before I would step any distance into the woods without a compass.

Farm Animals in the Woods: Chickens, a Pig

A long cold winter dragged at our spirits. The snow-banks were high and cold winds whipped across the lake. We dreamt of warm spring days and ways to ease our economic struggle. Mother decided we could grow garden vegetables, have a few chickens and maybe a pig.

While waiting for spring Mother ordered baby chicks. They arrived when the snow was still heavy on the ground — a hundred tiny balls of yellow and black down. Mother kept them behind the kitchen stove well off the floor, covered with a light wool blanket. They cheeped constantly, pecked at their parcels of ground grain and grew. Soon it was evident that more suitable housing would have to be found for them. I cut and peeled logs and built a stockade-type chicken house. I chinked the cracks with moss gathered from the woods, installed two windows and a door facing south. Out in front I made a pen of fine mesh wire for the chicks when they were large enough to be out on their own.

Soon after we moved our budding flock to their new quarters, a skunk beheld this palatial home, so conveniently stocked with food and determined to acquire squatters' rights. I set several traps hoping to get the skunk and not a chicken. My efforts were successful . . . in a way. The morning after I caught the skunk, I opened the door and found the chickens high on their roosts, gasping. The skunk was defiant; the air was heavy and overpowering. I shot the skunk, but I wasn't sure that I was the victor. Long after the place had been aired and whitewashed, that potent odor returned each rainy day, like a reincarnation of a long lost soul surging back and forth within the confines of the building.

The chickens grew larger. I bought more wire fencing. That summer we enjoyed the fruits of our labors. Almost any day I could be seen coming down the hill toward the lodge dangling beheaded chickens. I sat in the backyard and plucked them, saving the feathers for pillows. Occasionally an unexpected puff of wind confronted my feather collection. Then elongated "snowflakes" lifted in a swirl, scattered and settled gently back to earth.

By keeping the chickens over the winter we had fresh eggs to supplement our diet and hens to mother a new batch of chicks the following spring. It was a cold winter. I banked the snow high against the chicken house, but in spite of my efforts, the chickens' combs froze and shriveled so it was difficult to tell a hen from a rooster.

In time the hens dutifully hatched their nests of eggs and strode around the yard with their ever growing chicks. Overconfident, I let them roam at will. They never strayed far; they pecked with abandon and scratched dirt with the hope of finding unsuspecting insects.

In the beginning of August the chickens were ready to be harvested. Mother suggested we wait just a little longer until they added another half pound or so. As I closed the chicken house one night, I had the feeling there were fewer birds than usual. Over the next two days it became evident that the flock was being depleted rapidly. A thorough search disclosed dead chickens scattered through the woods like seeds dropped by the wind. Every chicken appeared unharmed, but on closer scrutiny I found two tiny holes on the neck — the mark of a weasel's stealthy job of killing. I killed the few remaining chickens, and we went out of the poultry business.

We bought a young piglet from a Cloquet farmer who was working as a logger nearby. He returned to his farm every weekend and on one trip brought back our pig. I built a tight pen and tied a couple of sled dogs in close proximity to discourage inquisitive bears. We fed the pig all the table scraps from the resort. She grew large and fat.

Time came for the pig to be slaughtered, but by now she was almost a pet. No one wanted to end the life of this friendly creature who had so effectively disposed of our garbage. Finally Dad said, "Enough of this nonsense, go get me the .22." I obediently brought the rifle and Dad stalked up the hill. Presently I heard a shot and the miserable squealing of the pig. Two more shots were followed by a loud call, "Just-e-e-e-n!"

I hightailed it up the hill and discovered Dad missed the shot below the ear and caught the jaw. I was greeted with, "Stick 'em, girl. Damn it stick 'em." The pig tore around the yard and I after it. Finally I stuck it in the throat with a knife. Dad said, "After it bleeds bring it down. We have to dip it in boiling water and get the hide cleaned of hair."

Eventually the pig was drained of its life blood. I loaded it into a wheelbarrow, took it to the cabin and, with the aid of a pulley, hung it from a tree. We put a washtub of water on the stove and stoked the firebox with wood. When the water boiled vigorously we carried the tub outside and lowered the pig into the scalding water. Dad said this would make it real easy to scrape off the hair.

We lifted the pig free of its bath after a thorough

soaking, and I took a hardwood stick with a sharpened edge and scraped and scraped. My most concerted effort had the same effect as a dull-bladed mower passing over a lawn — the grass bends over and pops right back up in the wake. I tried scraping with the edge of my hunting knife, and when that too failed, I went after Dad's safety razor and shaved the hanging form from top to bottom. It took several razor blades but it did work.

I never did learn the accepted manner of doing the job, but then that was our first and last pig. The pig furnished us with lard, pork roasts, pork chops and sausage. Mother frequently spoke of the merits of pork sausage put down in lard and the zest it added to venison hamburgers, which she remembered from her childhood on an Illinois farm.

There was one additional benefit from keeping that pig. It did a superb job of rooting tomato seeds into the ground. The following summer the pig pen was a solid tomato patch yielding bushels of green tomatoes which we canned.

A Try at Gardening

Since Mother grew up on a farm, she felt we were wasting a great potential of food by not gardening. The soil at her childhood home was black and rich with exceptional productivity. Our "soil" was the result of earthmoving glaciers and the cycling of forest growth: rocks, interspersed with decayed leaves and humus. We moved boulders and cleared trees from a patch of land. An axe and crosscut saw were our weapons to fell and cut up the trees. A few sticks of dynamite blew the stumps.

Painstakingly Dad cleared the land and removed the rocks and boulders, which eventually made a neat rock fence around two sides of the garden plot. Each year Dad harvested a new supply of rocks. In spring as frost left the ground, it would lift the rocks a few inches and let a little dirt sift under them until they surfaced.

Warm May days are an enticing and deceptive lure for spading, staking rows and planting virulent seeds. Woe to those who fall for the decoy. Within one or two days in May, a seemingly nourishing rain may turn to snow, as aging winter reluctantly turns over the reins to the seething youth of spring. The first week of June, when mosquitoes and blackflies are in their full blown glory, is the appropriate planting time. Growth of our garden was rapid as garden seeds go, and we watched with pleasure as the sprouts grew successfully higher.

Then one morning all that remained was a two-inch stubble as if a mower had passed that way. Careful examination revealed tell-tale hoof prints of a few deer who had enjoyed a meal of fresh greens the night before. The deer became accustomed to our sled dogs tied around the edge of the garden; they seemed to sense that the dogs could go only a certain distance and no further. Dad discovered that the odor from mothballs placed around the garden's perimeter served us as well as a scarecrow rigged in a corn patch.

Dad tried all kinds of experiments to overcome the short growing season. (Short season hybrid seeds were not available yet.) Strawberries (which eventually produced 125 quarts), raspberries (which the bear periodically investigated), carrots, asparagus, pie plant, onions and radishes grew proficiently. Tomatoes seldom ripened, and sweet corn developed into a few edible ears. Potatoes were particularly prolific, and cucumbers made excellent small pickles when we were able to outsmart the family of groundhogs who moved into the patch. During July and particularly August the garden amply provided the fresh vegetables and lettuce needed for the lodge.

Dad's Garden and Mother's Chicken House

Consolidation and Survival

Father was a heavy stockholder in a bank in Barrington, Illinois. During the financial panic of 1930 a run was made on "his" bank, and it was forced to close. At that time stockholders were subject to double indemnity. Consequently our homes in Barrington and Lake Zurich were sold to help pay the creditors. We had no home in Illinois, nor was there money available to continue my graduate work. We had no choice but to move to Gunflint.

Mother bought this fishing camp for summer operation — not to make it our home. She had to give up her roots and creative activities in Barrington. From the challenges and social life in the academic world, I was thrust into an area where living was an endless struggle. Radio

73

reception was poor and television was unheard of. The lodge had neither electricity nor inside plumbing. There were so many differences which called for new adjustments: the remoteness, the hilly narrow winding gravel road, the forestry phone on which long distance calls could not be charged, lack of mail and freight service, Indian neighbors, canoe trips, fishing and the dog teams.

Father came to Gunflint in 1933, crushed from his financial losses. Although he took no direct part in the business, he found a productive nitch in fishing, telling stories to the guests and gardening.

Not many people could afford to take vacations during these times of economic stress, and this influenced our resort operation. Fewer guests hired guides, and the fur prices dropped. Both of these factors affected the livelihood of our Indian neighbors. Joe Blackjack took his family to Atikokan, Ontario and Eddie Burnside went to the Indian reservation at Red Lake. Abie Cook took his family to Grand Marais and later to Duluth where food was being dispensed to those in need. Mike Deschampe and Billy Connors went to Saganaga. Pete Spoon left for Kashabowie, Ontario and Mike Powell took his family to Grand Marais. That left Charlie Cook and his mother Mary, on Gunflint Lake. The Plummer family — Walter, George, Awbutch and their mother Netowance — moved to Magnetic Bay. The men who remained on Gunflint guided for us and Awbutch Plummer worked at the lodge.

It was Mother's dogged determination and steadfastness that brought us through the first crucial years. Our expansion of the lodge properties had been inopportune, and we were unable to meet our obligations. We survived because Dora Blankenburg carried our mortgage as long as we paid the interest. A. M. Anderson, president of Grand Marais State Bank, told the creditors to hold off and I would eventually pay them in full. The heads of my creditors' firms agreed to carry my accounts if I paid what I could each month. I doubt if such considerations would be given now, but present times are not comparable to the times of the depression, when the stock market was uncontrolled and innumerable businesses were failing.

Mother and I shared the tasks of operating the resort. She was the hostess, she answered all correspondence (in longhand), planned the meals and supervised the help. I took over the ordering, paying bills, keeping the canoes, boats and all equipment in repair. I have often been asked how I knew how to repair motors. I answered, "I took them apart to find out how they functioned and to discover what part wasn't working."

Eventually the Duluth man who sold us our Saganaga island would wait no longer. We lost the island and our improvements which made it a comfortable outpost.

CHAPTER 4

"MARRIAGE AND DAILY LIFE"

Marriage

IN 1932 Bill Kerfoot came to work for us. He and his sister Margaret had been guests at Gunflint Lodge and at our Saganaga island. He managed a dude ranch in South Dakota for his brother Paul until the ranch folded as a result of the depression. Bill came to Gunflint seeking work. Although we couldn't afford hiring extra help, he agreed to work for a pittance and room and board.

After Bill spent two years as a "handyman," he and I decided to combine forces. His total asset was an old Model T Ford and mine was part interest in a debt ridden lodge. He had plans to return to his home in St. Paul and shingle the roof on his mother's house that fall. Suddenly on one trip to Grand Marais we decided to get married. A preacher obliged by performing the ceremony; Bill already had the license, but I had been dragging my feet on making this commitment. Since we had no money for a honeymoon, we continued on to St. Paul and worked together on reroofing his mother's house.

Mother Kerfoot, a small spicy woman, greeted me with some trepidation. She called my attention to the dozen mounted pictures lined up on the piano — the girls Bill had fallen in love with, proposed to and almost married. The girls were all beautifully attired and perfectly groomed.

I, slight of build, arrived in a pair of blue jeans, a wool plaid shirt and a short haircut.

Bill and I started the renovation job the next day. After we had been climbing ladders and pounding nails for a day or two, Mother Kerfoot came out of the house to see how we were progressing. She beheld her new daughter-in-law sitting astride the ridgepole smoking a cigarette. She tottered back to the house and took to her bed where she remained until we had finished. She, the wife of a man who preached for a number of years and then became president of Hamline University, could visualize the neighbors peeking from behind their curtains and exchanging bits of gossip. After we completed the job, we bade her adieu at her bedside.

There is a time when children are planned for . . . and then there are times! On a snowy late fall day in 1935 our first child was about to be born a month early. We called Dr. Hicks, our local Grand Marais doctor who regularly traveled by snowshoe and dog team to wherever he was needed in the country. He had performed successful operations on improvised kitchen tables in distant log cabins with the most meager of supplies.

On this occasion, Dr. Hicks hired a driver to accompany him over the rocky, hilly roads to Gunflint on a blustery, snowy November night. After Dr. Hicks arrived and made the examination, he said, "We better be heading for Duluth and get as far as we can." Bill and I followed him in our car, stopping periodically for the doctor to make another check. Each time he decided we could go farther. We finally made it to Two Harbors, the first hospital available, where he called a halt.

Our first son, Neil Tad, was born in a hospital room where there were no special facilities for a mother or a one-month premature baby. An oxygen tent was loaned by a dentist in Duluth. The staff had difficulty in keeping the baby's temperature constant. After 10 days Neil Tad found the struggle for survival too great a challenge.

The winter stayed desperately cold, week after week. When it is 30 to 40 below zero, the cold seems to seep through cracks where cracks didn't exist. It seeps in around window casings and through floors. Physically I had fallen to pieces. Bill spent hours with me playing cards, cribbage and encouraging me to rise from my depression. Lying in our cold bedroom off the lodge kitchen, all I could think of was a warm sunny place on a southern beach. Bill's infinite patience and the curative measures of nature created my recovery.

We worked together, trying to carry on a sustaining business. At this time our finances ran precariously low, and we grabbed at any proposition to help carry us through.

About then the St. Paul Winter Carnival was in its infancy. The Davidson Properties Company, owners of the building which housed the St. Paul Pioneer Press, offered to sponsor my dog team as a part of their carnival marching unit.

Some drivers took their dog teams on these circuits all winter. Their dogs were hitched in pairs. They were well trained in city work and pranced in perfect unison to the drum beat of the marching units.

Bill and I weighed the odds carefully. Our dogs had never been out of the woods and were trained to pull hard and travel at a steady fast pace over lakes and snowshoe trails. We had never driven dogs in the city. Although the remuneration was not great, it would help carry us over those few crucial months. We accepted.

On January 30, 1937 we set out for St. Paul. We loaded Egi in the trunk by himself because he picked fights with the other dogs. We filled the sled with harnesses and tied it on top of the car. We piled the rest of the dogs in the car, in the back seat and on the floor. One of us drove while the other rode facing backward ready to rap the first dog that emitted a complaining growl. Unpredictably, the dogs would either flop against each other sublimely or at the slightest provocation become a snarling, nipping, melee of teeth and fur. We remained in constant alert and managed the trip to St. Paul with only minor skirmishes. An unused warehouse was designated as the dogs' quarters. We stayed with Mother Kerfoot, who by this time had wholeheartedly accepted me, her newest daughter-in-law, as long as I did not smoke in her home.

Much to our chagrin we discovered the city streets were almost dry. We had a set of small wheels attached to the undercarriage of our sled's runners. Our brake was a large hinged contraption on the back of the sled, held off the ground by a door spring, with the free end filed into two sharp points. This unit was very effective in snow, but on the St. Paul streets it left a wake of sparks.

Each morning the dogs had to run off their penned up exuberance before they were manageable. My lead dog John, nervous in this new environment, was oblivious to all traffic and plowed straight ahead. If it hadn't been Carnival week, and if the drivers of motorized vehicles hadn't been both considerate and cautious, we no doubt would have been squashed into small pieces. In desperation I located a large cemetery nearby. We ran all the roads within this confine. If there were a ghost hovering over its last resting place, we probably had an appreciative audience, who in that release, may have been carried back to its childhood.

On parade day we lined up and started the long slow procession which was not the normal pace that John traveled. In spite of all our efforts he regularly took the team into the center of the marching unit ahead of us. If left to his own devices, he surely would have pushed his way through all the units and led the procession.

We drafted four enthusiastic youngsters from the crowd to hang onto ropes attached to the sled and restrain the dogs. No doubt we made quite a spectacle, with the dogs pulling, the sparks flying and the youngsters hanging onto ropes on each side of the sled, while we slipped and slid in an effort to keep the team in place. If only I could have disciplined a couple of the dogs, they would have steadied down. But we had been warned that members of the SPCA would raise a ruckus. One of our friends slipped us a quirt, which served effectively as a threat.

As a part of our obligation, we were asked to take our team to the Davidsons' home located on a hill overlooking St. Paul. The Davidsons' children and their schoolmates wanted dog team rides. We drove up the long hill with John ignoring all traffic, stoplights and screeching tires. We were met by a chauffeur driving a large limousine filled with excited youngsters. We mushed up and down the streets, block after block, with the limousine stopping at our side now and again to exchange groups of youngsters.

Upon our return home we decided, never again. But the next year the proposition was made. Our financial position was tight, so we accepted the challenge. This time we were better prepared and far wiser.

We Build a Log Home

Bill and I wanted our own log home. We planned to spend the winter building it, so we practiced the previous spring by building a small log guest cabin. We felt confident that we had learned the basic construction techniques.

Bill peeled the logs to a golden hue, until every trace of bark was gone. I hewed and fitted the logs according to instructions in a book — which book I kept well-hidden to avoid being kidded by the occasional trapper stopping in to inspect our progress. (Most trappers were excellent woodsmen skilled in the art of building tight cabins.)

To begin we hunted large, comparatively straight aspen. We felled the trees and limbed them with an axe. Then we cut the logs in lengths with a double crosscut saw. We hauled the logs with our dog team. One end of the log was roped onto our toboggan to keep it from digging into the snow. By rough-peeling the portion of the log that extended beyond the toboggan, we could make it skid fairly easily.

The logs for our home, however, were much longer and heavier than those we used in the cabin. As I hauled a log off the nearby hill and started over the crest, I had a difficult time holding the log back so a catapulting outfit wouldn't overtake the dogs, who were running as fast as they could go. Although they quickly learned, when they were being overtaken, to step to one side and let the

Log Guest Cabin that Bill and I Built

toboggan zip by and drag them down the hill backwards — an outcome preferable to being clobbered by the long heavy log.

Bill peeled the logs meticulously and rolled them into a large pile, which we hoped would be sufficient for the job. We marked each new log with a pair of scribers to fit the one below it. Then we hewed out a groove between the markings, laid a strip of oakum along the groove which acted as a sealer and rolled the log into place. If it were marked correctly and hewed to the line it would fit like a glove. We used no nails because as the timbers dried they would settle and retain their solid structure.

We hewed our floor joists and slipped them into pre-cut notches in the first base log. The walls followed. We progressed log by log, with Bill building the south wall and I the north — we overlapped on the corners.

By spring we had our home finished except the roof. We hastily covered a small alcove which would just hold a bed and hung a mosquito bar across the front. Then we

Our Log Home

had a place of our own which we did not have to give up to incoming guests.

Diplomacy

The people who operated resorts on the Trail were independent, ingenious and self-sustaining. Each operator competed for the scattered tourists who took their cars over the rocky, hilly roads to reach the inland border lakes. Lodge signs were scattered along the Trail and concentrated, in assorted sizes, at each side road. The lodge entrances at the lower end of the Trail were burdened with signs from all the resorts beyond. Signs on the Trail began to look like roadside advertising approaching a honky-tonk city. Signs were sometimes taken down by one resort owner and thrown into the woods, but eventually retrieved and replaced by the sign owner.

Into this atmosphere Bill offered the suggestion that we all get together to try to solve some of our joint problems. I thought he was wasting his time, but he persisted and a meeting was called at Gateway Lodge. Everyone came — the Gilbertsons from Greenwood, the Boostroms from Clearwater, the Gapens from Hungry Jack, the Brandts from Poplar Lake, the Kerfoots from Gunflint (us), and the Blankenburgs from Sea Gull. They came partly in a defensive mood with their hackles ready to rise, and partly to see what we newcomers were trying to do.

First Bill presented our mutual problems, then we had an open discussion. We discovered we had been "had" — not by each other but by the public. The incoming guests were aware of our lack of cooperation. When one resort quoted a price of accommodations or boat rentals, the guests claimed a lower price was being offered at another resort. The first resort would match the lower price to get the business. We had all fallen for this maneuver, and the result was we all were barely eking out a living and making very little profit.

We agreed to remove the unsightly signs along the Trail and post one sign for each resort at its spur entrance. We worked together to place groups of mileage signs along the road every 15 miles.

This then in 1935 was the beginning of the Gunflint Trail Association, an organization that grew stronger and became a united and cooperative group. Our successes did not come without debate. We faced some controversial problems, and working out solutions to our mutual benefit often took time.

As new resorters joined the Association they too were instilled with cooperation and our pride in keeping the Trail and the surrounding woods a treasured area.

Deer Hunters, 1937

Each November our main source of income was hosting deer hunters. We usually hunted with success in the immediate vicinity of the lodge. In 1936, however, the deer herd was being depleted, due to deep snows, wolves and hunting. The Department of Game and Fish closed deer hunting at our end of the Trail for two years to give the herd a better chance.

In 1937 we were taking our guests by car to Clearwater Lake and then by dog team along the old railroad bed to

Deer Hunters with Booty, early 1940s
Two Guests, Myself, Guest, Bill and Dad

the far end of Daniels Lake where we had set up a camp under canvas.

Two large tents sufficed for the sleeping quarters and one additional tent served as a combined kitchen and mess hall. Our camp crew consisted of Art Smith as guide, Bill to help set up and maintain the camp, Marjorie Cole to help in the kitchen and I was cook. We had breakfast at daylight, carried lunches, and supper was at dark. In the interim we all went hunting. There were twelve hunters, some more skilled or luckier than others. And all the game bagged was shared equally. We hauled the deer to Clearwater by dog team. After a hard day's hunt it was not unusual for a deer to wander close to camp at night and snort in defiance.

During our stay at the camp, we constructed a log raft with Art Smith's help, and we rigged it so we could attach a small outboard motor. We tied the raft at the far

85

The Raft on Daniels Lake

end of the lake for our return. Inevitably, in fishing or hunting, we travel to the other side of the lake or over the next hill in pursuit of our sport.

One late afternoon almost at dusk, Marjorie, Bill and I were making our last raft trip back to camp. Darkness came rapidly, the temperature dropped and a full moon rose over the hills, reflecting a long beam across the calm water of Daniels Lake. As we chugged down the middle of the lake, we became aware that the lake was rapidly glazing over. The new ice climbed the front of the raft threatening to submerge us. Bill constantly shoved ice off the front as we inched our body weight forward. We broke ice this way until we were close to camp, where a two-night freeze extended out 25-30 feet. This ice would carry our weight. That night the entire lake froze solid.

The next morning we hauled the hunters and all their gear to the road head by dog team. By afternoon we started breaking camp. John, our experienced lead dog, hauled load after load over the three-night freeze close to shore where travel was safe. Camp was cleared and the fire was extinguished. All that remained was for Fuzzy, a leader in training, to follow John's tracks and bring the second team to the outgoing trail.

Fuzzy started with gusto and ignored his commands. Instead of following the shore, he headed out across the lake. He crossed from the three-night freeze onto new ice, and it suddenly gave way. The five-dog team clawed for a foothold, mixing up the harnesses more with each struggle. I hollered to Bill for a rope. I crept out on the shore ice with a long pole. I hooked a harness with the pole and, lifting and pulling at the same time, I tried to pull one dog up on the ice. When I gave one mighty heave, the ice I was sitting on gave way. I joined the dogs in their icy, churning melee.

Bill came running up the shore with a rope. He threw one end to me, and I tied it around my wrist. As he pulled on the rope, the ice broke for several feet. But he was finally able to pull me atop, and the ice held. All the while I held onto one dog harness, so as I emerged, so did the team — almost. One dog had been trampled under and drowned.

We rebuilt the fire and retrieved dry clothes from packs. While I was driving the dogs back to Clearwater I first realized the seriousness of this close call. When I arrived at Clearwater Lodge, Petra Boostrom took one look at my makeshift attire and intuitively knew I had gone through the ice. She said, "Well now, you better sit down and have some hot coffee."

The following year the Game and Fish Department reopened deer season at our end of the Trail, so our guests could hunt in our own backyard. Even so the deer hunting routine kept me going at a fast pace. We got up long before daylight, started fires, packed lunches, made breakfast, cleaned cabins, helped make a couple of deer drives and returned in time to start supper.

After this particular deer season in 1938, I went to Duluth in mid-December and after a few days' wait, gave birth to a son — Bruce.

The Wood Supply

We had a big wood burning cook stove in the kitchen and airtight stoves for heat in the cabins. They were all hungry for wood. Our available supply was either aspen, which burned clean but did not hold a fire, or birch loaded with sap. The birch gave more heat and carried well overnight, but when burned green, it formed a tarry creosote residue which dripped at the stovepipe elbows and ran down the joints.

The ideal in heating with wood is to cut and stack it a year ahead so it is dry and produces maximum heat. Bill and I seldom reached that goal. Unconsciously we had slipped into the ways of the Indians. They seldom stacked wood for the future but cut it on an almost daily basis. For me cooking with green wood was most frustrating. But Bill postponed wood cutting chores as long as possible.

Wood is handled many times before it is finally burned. We cut the wood in eight-foot lengths and loaded it onto our truck. We hauled it to an area near our stationary saw, and there we cut it into stove lengths.

Cutting wood with a stationary saw as we did is dangerous, for the slightest miscalculation can cut off a hand or arm. The saw blade is mounted on one end of a mandrel, at the other end is a cast iron flywheel to counter the action of the saw. We powered our saw by a belt running from a rear wheel of Bill's Ford. When the car was revved up, the saw hummed.

Bill and I developed a smooth rhythm, and we never allowed anyone else to operate the saw. I worked at the tilting tray, pulling the log forward the right distance and pushing it into the whirling blade. Bill always worked at the saw, holding the log as it was cut and throwing the pieces on the growing pile.

After the wood was cut into stove lengths, the pieces were split, hauled to and stacked near the cabin where they would be used. Then they were carried, as needed, to a woodbox near the stove, and finally thrown into the stove. Each stick was handled eight times.

Inevitably, before spring arrived, we ran out of wood. Bill trudged off to the woods puffing on his pipe, with a single crosscut saw swaying uneasily on his shoulder. Once again we had misjudged the amount of wood we would need for the winter.

Bill — Going for Wood

Cooks

The quality of our firewood affected the temperament of the cook who worked for us, and the quality of a cook spelled success or failure for any resort serving meals. The first few years we had some excellent cooks — housewives from Grand Marais who were willing to cook for a summer "back in the woods." But they never stayed longer than a year or two, as the demands of their families required them to return home. Later we went through a series of professional cooks — men, women and couples who had one thing in common — for the most part they were temperamental prima donnas.

Finding cooks for the season was always difficult. One spring three resorts on the Trail — Gunflint Lodge, End of the Trail Lodge and Swanson's Lodge — were all hunting new applicants. Mother Bunn, who with her son Walt owned and operated Swanson's Lodge, found Mrs. S — a good cook who did not quite fit their needs. They referred her to us, but we had already hired Mrs. B. We passed Mrs. S on to Al Hedstrom, owner and operator of End of the Trail Lodge, who hired her.

The week before our Mrs. B was to arrive, our previous cook wrote she wanted to return, bringing a friend Mrs. T as second cook. We wanted our previous cook back, so we hired Mrs. B as second cook and referred Mrs. T to End of the Trail Lodge where Al had just received word that Mrs. S was cancelling out. Al hired Mrs. T only to learn a day later that his previous cook wanted to return. Al called Mrs. T and switched her to second cook.

About that time Mrs. B (our second cook) cancelled out, so Al offered Mrs. T (his second cook) back to us. Meanwhile Mrs. T received a raise and decided to stay where she was.

Butchie, Aggie and Sharon in Front of the Lodge

Somehow out of all this we hired Agnes Lanktree Jackson for the summer.

There was only one Aggie — such a composite that she defies description. She was with us for a dozen years, then as she grew older she returned to cook for a month in the spring and fall and over the Christmas holiday season.

Before Aggie came to us, she had cooked in road or logging camps for most of her life. Her dad ran many of the camps for road crews building the Gunflint Trail. One of the last camps he managed was at Lanktree Lake — named after him. (In recent years some enterprising forester who had no regard for the history of the area had it changed, and it is now recorded on maps as Extortion Lake.)

Aggie's day in the logging camps started at four in the morning. Breakfast was required on the table at five; men left for the woods by six. At ten Aggie rode a horse to the work area with coffee and cookies. She hurried back to her cook house to prepare a noonday meal, then delivered coffee again in the afternoon and returned to cook a big supper at night.

Aggie also baked all the bread, pies and cookies besides cooking the meals and somehow had time to spare. Her only help was a "bull cook" who brought in wood for the cook stove and kept the kitchen clean.

Through the years in these camps she acquired loggers' habits: a vocabulary full of expletory words, incessant smoking and the ability to drink large quantities of beer without perceptible effects.

We had fast rules at the resort. No one was allowed to smoke while on the job; Aggie chain smoked all the time. No one was allowed to take pop or beer without accounting for it; Aggie helped herself at will, not with the thought of stealing, just as her due.

Aggie worked hard for long hours, doing what was needed. She would tote a tray of tasty food to Mother's cabin if she knew Mother was ailing. Or she'd change the babies' diapers or give them bottles of formula when they squalled. To her, anyone who put in less than 14-16 hours a day, or left the kitchen before it was spick-and-span with all the work done, was a lazy "son of a bitch." All the waitresses, cabin girls and outside boys, most of whom were of high school or college age, came under that category in Aggie's eyes.

Each morning I appeared in the kitchen by six. Aggie had preceded me by an hour. She'd have breakfast ready, and her usual comment was, "Well Jesus Christ I thought you were going to sleep all day."

We learned from her how to build a screen-enclosed outbuilding for hanging fresh quarters of beef as was done in logging camps. The meat formed an outer crust and slowly aged, becoming more tender each day.

When our calf Ferdinand had a distended belly, and we didn't know what to do for it, she yelled, "Jesus Christ, throw it and sit on its head." I followed her instructions, and she grabbed the calf by the tail to swing its hindquarters back and forth and periodically thump them on the ground. Aggie's treatment was a success, and the calf resumed its normal size.

One fall when Bill was away for a period of time, Aggie said "Burning green wood is a bunch of god-damned nonsense." She turned to me and said, "Sharpen that double crosscut saw and come with me." We had ample trees for wood on our back forty, so with the long two-handled crosscut saw and an axe we set out for the woods.

We used the axe to fell and then limb trees that stood 60-70 feet high. Together we sawed them in appropriate lengths. I learned the rhythm of sawing — pull-coast, pull-coast, hour after hour. Aggie and I sawed and split enough wood for the entire season — we had a pile of wood as high as a haystack. When the job was finished, Aggie sat in the kitchen smoking a cigarette as if she had just been out on a playful romp. I felt stiff all over.

Aggie was someone special. Loyal and hard-working, she was a rare find who was never duplicated. Long after she could no longer work she remained a friend.

Eventually there came a day in 1939, while Bill was away at some political meetings, that I found myself out of wood. I took the truck and drove to the wood lot. With my one-year-old son Bruce hanging from the side of the truck in his tick-a-noggin, I went to work cutting a load of wood. Right then I decided to convert to fuel oil stoves in the cabins. The burning of fuel oil eliminated that demanding task, but to this day I much prefer the smell of burning wood.

Hiring a good cook and putting up wood were only two of many facets of a resort operation in a wilderness. Another problem was communication.

Gunflint Trail Telephone Associates

In 1924 the only communication line available to the resorts along the Gunflint Trail was the telephone line strung to fire towers owned and maintained by the State of Minnesota. This line was a single telephone wire hung to trees by split insulators with wire ties.

The state line serviced a few resorts as far up the Trail as Gunflint Lodge to facilitate their fire reporting. As new resorts were built there were increased demands for phone service until the line was loaded with seven resorts. These were in addition to the fire towers, which always had priority use. Later the fire towers gradually converted to radio, and the towers used the telephone less and less. The state became disinterested in maintaining the circuit, and we were in a quandary.

The existing resorts met and formed the Gunflint Trail Telephone Associates with all the bylaws and registrations required by the state. The Associates then purchased the line from the state. More resorts were added until the line served 10 parties, which was deemed its ultimate capacity. The line was tied into the Bell system at Grand Marais. Each resort on the 10-party line had its own coded ring.

The line was as frail as a gossamer thread. It became customary when traveling up and down the Trail to watch for fallen trees on the line and stop to chop them or push them off. We carried spare wire, pliers and an axe in our car at all times.

Maintenance on the line was apportioned among the resorts, each being responsible for hanging insulators on their assigned stretch of line.

Sometimes more than one insulator was torn free, and the line sagged to the ground. On one occasion a moose sauntered into the barrier and stretched the wire so taut it

94

broke. The moose kept going with a long trail of wire extending helter skelter through the woods. Sometimes a large tree would fall with such a whop (through the endeavors of a beaver or blown by the wind) that the line would snap.

The first resorter to come along always patched a break. To pull the wire ends together we hooked one end of the wire to the bumper of our car and drove ahead to stretch that side taut. Then we would drag the other end by hand as close as we could to the attached end and fill the remaining gap with a wire splice. Later we would return with come-a-longs, sleeves, crimpers and a ladder to replace the makeshift patch and retie the line to the insulators.

It was not uncommon for a resort operator to greet an arriving guest while hanging from a ladder or fixing an insulator.

Three people were especially instrumental in solving phone problems during this period.

Petra Boostrom at Clearwater Lodge became a relay station. She was a busy mother and resort hostess, but she always helped relay our rings with gracious good humor. Many times she tied a baby in a high chair, shoved cooking food to the back of the stove and helped crank, in unison, on the phone. No matter how frequently she was asked to help she never hesitated. The Boostroms were located halfway to town, so their ringing help would usually carry us through. But if she and I weren't successful in getting the ring to carry through to town, she would call Gapens at Hungry Jack and the three of us would ring together. That frequently worked.

Mrs. Mollison was the Grand Marais telephone operator who relayed long distance messages in and out. Sometimes only her indefatigable effort succeeded in getting the messages through.

A typical conversation with Molly went like this:
"Molly, send telegram."
"O.K."
"Have accommodations."
"Can't get that, repeat."
"Have accommodations."
"Can't get it, spell."
"H, as in Harry."
"Try again."
"H, as in Howard."
"Try again."
"H, as in Hell."
"Got it."

Amid the crackling and static on the line, Molly laboriously and with infinite patience decoded our messages and sent them on their way.

If one received a laurel for service before, during and after the 1936 forest fires, Molly would have worn a golden crown set with precious jewels. The forest fires were burning out of control, and we resorters were at constant alert, responsible for our guests' safety. She attended her switchboard for hours on end to send us the latest updates on threatened areas.

Finally there was Al Fenstad, the manager of the Northwestern Bell exchange in Grand Marais. He gave us advice. He loaned us tools and telephone equipment. Often his donation of a piece of wire scrounged from some abandoned line kept our little telephone company in operation.

When Al first loaned me a pair of climbers and a belt, I had some reservations. I was successful at climbing, but while I was at the pole's top I leaned slightly forward. The spurs became disengaged from the green tree bark, and I came slithering to the ground feeling like a porcupine with newly-acquired quills.

Our 50-mile single circuit telephone line became efficient when everything was frozen during the winter months. Once when Mother and I were coming back from town we found a break. We had no wire along, so we filled the gap with an old tire chain. The chain transmitted messages, both local and long distance for several weeks until we repaired the break.

But in summer, rain dripping from the trees created a thousand grounds; the line crackled with static. When this grounded condition was at its worst, it took the three of us — Petra Boostrom, Gapens and us — ringing together to get the operator. Sometimes we had to give up and wait for a day with more favorable weather conditions.

In the mid-40s the U.S. Forestry installed a metallic circuit on real telephone poles all the way to the end of the Trail. Bearskin, Sea Gull and Chik Wauk were the only resorts allowed on the line at first, and they were only allowed limited use. In 1946 the 10 resorts of the Gunflint Trail Telephone Associates joined together to buy 120 miles of new copper wire and necessary hardware for a new line. The Associates leased space on the federal poles and, using trucks and manpower from Northwestern Bell, erected the new metallic circuit.

With this upgrading the reception drastically improved. Maintenance, still apportioned among the resorts, was easier even though it now entailed two lines, the transmission line and the return ground. The lines alternated in attachment between every so many poles. On a windy day they had an inclination to wrap around each other in a close embrace, putting our line out of order.

When an emergency message had to get through, I climbed onto a high hillock and tapped the federal line on the poles. This procedure was a bit unorthodox, and we used it sparingly.

The operator did not always fully comprehend the conversation, which might go like this:

"Operator, I would like to make a long distance call and charge it to Gunflint Lodge."

"Madam, those circuits are busy. I will call you back."

"I'm sorry but I am not at the number I'm charging to because that line is temporarily out of order."

"What phone are you calling from, and I will call you back on that number."

"This phone doesn't have a number on this line."

"I don't understand."

"Well, you see, I am sitting on a high rock on a hill, under the telephone line which I have tapped in order to get this emergency call through."

"You are where!!?"

"Repeat."

"The circuits are no longer busy and I will place your call now."

At Gunflint Lodge we were at the end of the line of the Gunflint Trail Telephone Associates. I became a purveyor of messages to those beyond us — Tuscarora Lodge, Borderland Lodge, Heston's Lodge and seven intermediate summer homes. To conserve time and expedite message delivery, our clustered group of neighbors used old wire from the original state fire line and strung a line through the woods for about 12 miles. This was known as the Bush Line.

Anyone attempting to contact one of those resorts or private homes would still call Gunflint, and we would call the party on the Bush Line and then relay the messages from one to the other. The intricacies of using the Bush Line threw more than one Duluth operator into a tizzy. But eventually they became so oriented that they too called it by name.

Later on, with some maneuvering and Al Fenstad's

help, we installed a switch to connect parties on the two lines. But we still had to do the relay ringing.

Ours was the most sophisticated Bush Line in the area, but other shorter lines quickly developed. Trout Lake Lodge was hooked to the Gilbert Bloomquist home five miles away. Golden Eagle Lodge was serviced through Bearskin Lodge. Forest Lodge was connected to Clearwater Lodge. On the federal line there was a relay to End of the Trail Lodge from Chik Wauk.

These bush lines circumnavigated many rules and the technical restrictions of 10 customers to a circuit. The lines made it easier for the resorts without service to communicate with the other resorts and the rest of the world.

Later I bought a complete army surplus telephone system including switchboard, accessory wire and phones. Then I installed a phone in each of my cabins and connected them to the switchboard. At the same time I added the Bush Line to the newly-acquired unit, resulting in better connections for our neighbors. This exchange was an effective stopgap for several years.

In May 1958 our Gunflint Trail Telephone Associates negotiated a sale to Northwestern Bell with a tollfree line to Grand Marais guaranteed. We were required to underwrite 45 phones for a year (or until that capacity was reached by other phone requests). So each resort took two phones, one commercial and one residential. After six months the demand for phone service had increased enough that we could drop our second phones. By 1959 the Trail telephones went on a dial system with many circuits loaded to capacity.

Looking back at what we've gained and lost, the greatest loss is due to automation — the operators are gone forever. Our personal contact with operators made our old telephone system a living thing.

Ice Harvest

When we carried a bucket of chipped ice to a cabin for evening cocktails, or packed fish in boxes mixed with sawdust and ice, our guests gave little thought to its origin. Our ice did not come in formed blocks from ice machines. We cut it from the lake in mid-winter and stored it in our ice house. The ice we put up in winter was the lodge's only refrigeration for the entire summer.

The ice house was close to the lake because we had to haul 25-30 tons of ice into it every winter. Ice houses varied in size from 8x10 to 14x14 with double walls 6-8 feet high, insulated with sawdust. There were two openings in the building. The front opening was of full door-size, and boards were placed across it as the ice house was filled. On the opposite wall was a large window-size opening where we shoveled in the sawdust.

When we first built our ice house a logging camp was located nearby. Truckloads of sawdust from the camp were hauled in and piled cone-shape next to the new building. We used the same sawdust year after year; seldom did it need replenishing. In other remote locations where sawdust was not available, sphagnum moss was used effectively as an insulator, but it deteriorated and had to be replaced each year.

For us the ice harvest started directly after New Year's. Our lake froze over in mid-December; the smaller lakes froze a couple of weeks sooner. We allowed 10 days for the ice to become safe, then we measured out the ice field. We located the field far enough out so the saw wouldn't hit bottom and in an area where the ice had frozen smooth. Now we would have to shovel the ice field after each new snow. A layer of snow insulated the ice and prevented it from freezing deeper. If the snow became heavy enough, it could flood the ice, creating a layer of slush ice, which does not have a lasting quality like clear blue ice. When we harvested the ice, we had to trim off and discard slush ice.

The ideal time for ice harvest was when we could estimate the ice's thickness at 19-20 inches. Often around that time Nature delighted in sweeping through with a bitter wind and temperatures of 20 below zero. Then we were in a bind: if we waited for warmer weather, the ice was thicker, heavier and much harder to handle. If the days turned even colder, the saw froze in the cut even as it was pulled up and down. Once we started the harvest, we had to continue until the ice house was filled.

As the Indians on the far shore noticed our first stirrings on the ice, they would start snowshoeing across the lake to help us. They gave us a hand each day, as a friendly gesture, until the job was done.

It usually took two or three days to harvest ice: saw the cakes, pull them into the ice house, break open the frozen sawdust pile and shovel the sawdust into the house, packing it around the edges of each layer. The ice harvest was work, but it was also a neighborly event in which we were all involved. And when we finished we sensed a feeling of accomplishment. As Alice Brandt of Poplar Lake said to me years later, "We had fun putting up ice, didn't we?" It was an annual challenge that we all accepted and dealt with.

The tools we used to put up ice were an axe, a spud bar, an ice chisel, an ice saw and two very large ice tongs. First we scratched a grid on the bare ice for guidelines to saw the cakes straight and of a manageable size. Next we chiseled a hole through the ice, large enough to insert the saw. A channel was then cut along one side of the field and broken out with a spud bar. The cakes were sawed along the guidelines and broken out. Then we used the tongs to drag the ice cakes out of the water, to the ice house and then up a wooden ramp leading to the inside of the building.

I always had a terrible urge to figure out a way to do a job without "bulling it." My successes were about 50-50. Bill shuddered when one of my inspirations was about to develop. He figured the job could be accomplished the regular way in less time than it took me to get all my rigging in place.

One time after shoveling the snow to make a road to the ice house, I attached one end of a long rope to the car, extended the rope via a set of pulleys through the ice house and out to the field where it was attached to the tongs. On signal I drove off with such speed that the ice skidded up the chute into the ice house and hit the outer wall with a thud. This system would have worked, but we were too far apart to receive signals fast enough to keep us from knocking the building apart with the cakes of ice. With reluctance I dismantled my contrivance and tried a new approach.

I hitched the dogs to my long toboggan and took them to the ice field. After we pulled the cakes from the water we slid them onto the toboggan. On command the dogs would pull the load of cakes to the chute. John, our lead dog, shortly learned to turn the team around as soon as the cakes were unloaded, take the team back to the ice hole, turn the team again and wait to be loaded for the return. I came out ahead with this system as long as the dogs cooperated.

Toward the end of the day the dogs would tire. As they turned to pass one another, one dog would be jostled, which would start a few complaining woofs and end in a glorious dog fight with dogs, harnesses and ropes all a tangled, snarling, nipping mess.

It is difficult to untangle such a melee of uncooperative

beasts. I tried throwing pepper in their faces so they would have to sneeze and couldn't bite, but usually the wind wafted the spice toward me. Finally I just waded in and pulled them apart, whereupon they lopped against each other completely exhausted.

Walter Plummer and Abie Cook took turns with Bill on the sawing, and Butchie helped me push the cakes up and place them in layers in the ice house. If I could place the ice cakes in the same arrangement as they were in the lake, every-thing would fit together snugly like an interlocked jigsaw puzzle. I had been trying to teach Butchie to read and write and to expand her use of English. Suddenly it dawned on me we were back to essentials that needed no expansion: "You pull; I push."

Putting up ice was hard and heavy work. The higher we stacked the ice in the ice house, the more confining the space. As we neared the top it became increasingly difficult to shovel sawdust into the foot-wide space between the ice and the walls.

Our ice harvest was a round robin effort of neighbors. Often John Clark, our trapper friend across the lake, would come over to help us. In turn we would help him put up his ice. After these jobs were completed, Bill and I along with one or two of our Indian neighbors, would go down the lake to fill Charlie Olson's small ice house.

Light Plant Idiosyncrasies

Our guests seemed to have a constant struggle with the gasoline lanterns we provided for light in the cabins. The lanterns' tiny generators were forever plugging, and the mantles disintegrated at the slightest touch. They required daily filling and cleaning as well as frequent pumping during the evening. We used kerosene lamps and candles as a backup.

In 1937 we bought a tiny gasoline-powered electric generating plant. We strung a couple of wires to Mother and Dad's sleeping cabin, so they could use one light bulb. The effect was like that of buying a new rug for a house. The rug immediately called for new curtains or another upgrading. Table lamps and bedside lamps were added.

Electricity became so attractive that within a few years we bought a windcharger. We mounted it on a 10-foot tower on our cabin's roof. We connected it to used car batteries in our basement and we basked in the luxury of a light. We listened with joy to the vibrating hum of the generator's rotating blades. Sometimes when the wind died down, we sat in the ominous silence wondering how long before the batteries would run down and dim our lights beyond usefulness.

The temptation was too great. We added lights for the kitchen, and then for the dining room, all to the little gasoline plant that supplied electricity to my folks' cabin. When I tried to stretch the load to include the lobby, the plant grunted and groaned and folded up and died.

The Hedstroms were expanding their electrical usage at their sawmill at the lower end of the Trail. They sold us the 32-volt DC outfit from Grandpa Hedstrom's house. It came complete with 16 large glass batteries. We changed all our accessories to direct current, including electric motors, light bulbs and irons. This plant supplied the kitchen, dining room, lobby and office as well as Mother and Dad's cabin. This generator was a "one lunger" which thumped steadily by the hour, but it had an avaricious appetite for gasoline.

Grand Marais mechanic Emil Hall serviced all the light plants along the Trail when there was a serious breakdown. He was the greatest improviser of all time. He never really ordered a new piece to replace an ailing part. He found a usable substitute in his store of old leftovers in his Grand Marais shop or among some discarded pieces at some other light plant where he had been working. Until the needed part could be replaced, he made the plant function, using bailing wire and a Rube Goldberg-like contraption he created. His type of repair work would drive a perfectionist mad. But I thought his ingenuity unsurpassable.

Following World War II the army sold all types of surplus equipment including some diesel light plants. We bought one, and by coincidence Art Schliep (who had purchased Clearwater Lodge from Charlie Boostrom) bought an identical unit for his resort. They were relatively inexpensive and came crated, unused and with ample spare parts.

We built a reinforced cement base for our new machine and built a shed over it. We connected the plant to a 500-gallon diesel tank with a copper line. We had a 5 kw diesel plant in operation giving us 5000 watts of power. Yippee!!

We wired all eight cabins and added an electric water pump, refrigerator, freezer and ice making machine. Again we had to ration electric use: we shut off the freezer while pumping water and unplugged the refrigerators while ironing clothes.

The muffled thump of the generator became an unconscious part of our lives, for it ran 24 hours a day. We were attuned to the throb, so the slightest fluctuation sent us to the rescue. In spite of signs in the cabins prohibiting electrical appliances, an occasional guest would plug in an electric percolator for an early cup of coffee. If the plant were already loaded, it would emit the same painful groans as a woman in labor with her first child. We would dash to the kitchen to turn off an appliance and then try to track down the culprit.

105

One cold mid-winter night we learned that diesel oil flowing into a running plant would slowly become sluggish, then gel, and the plant would stop abruptly.

Repairs were continuous. Our plant had a small access plate on one side which gave admittance to the cylinder and revolving shaft. My two hands and the necessary tools completely filled the hole, so I had to make repairs with a sensitive touch and knowledge of the motor's innards. Needed parts were exchanged and re-exchanged with Art Schliep until both machines were combinations of the two. When either of our plants broke down, there would be a frantic phone call describing the part needed. Then starting from our resorts 25 miles apart, we'd drive toward each other and meet somewhere in the middle with the part.

Since the Gunflint Trail had no community supplier of electricity, resorters applied for power through the REA (Rural Electrification Association) — a government program providing electricity to farmers in rural America. Carlyle Campbell, our county agent at the time, worked diligently with REA officials, making surveys and trying to establish and prove our needs.

It seemed each time I was elbow-deep in grease, doing major repairs on our overloaded plant, Carlyle Campbell appeared with an REA agent who would ask, "If you had electricity available would you use more than you are using now? Do you think there is a real future potential?"

Even with our constant struggles to generate more power, none of us realized the demand for electricity that the advent of the REA would fulfill.

Eventually an REA co-op was formed. A group from the Trail served, along with several people from the North Shore of Lake Superior, on the board of directors of the Arrowhead Electric Co-op. Ernie Simon, a dedicated man, was hired to operate the co-op with business offices at Lutsen. Contracts were let, and the construction of distribution lines slowly proceeded. Everyone on the Trail tried to caress their light plants into living just a little longer, until we could all be hooked into the new system.

Art Schliep broke his wrist and discovered a latent talent of his wife's which she had kept well concealed. He sat on a nearby stump with his hand in a cast and gave Lavern instructions in winter maintenance on the light plant. She ably handled monkey wrenches, nuts, bolts and wiring blocks, but she began to wish she really were Minnie Moosemeat with her sister Tillie Beargrease, living on Mountain Lake — imaginary persons she dreamt up once when confronted by a couple of drunks. Her reverie was cut short when Art instructed her to clean the carburetor, jig up the generator, add oil and struggle with cold bolts.

We all worked furiously into the winter of 1958 to pamper our power plants a little longer. In late February a local pilot took the contractor and Ernie Simon on several trips flying over the power line to check it out. Ernie Simon said he anticipated a permanent energizing of the line on March 1, or at least he'd bust a button trying. By that date he expected to have the meters installed at sites where electrical inspection had been completed.

During one of these inspection flights, Eve Blankenburg set a raisin pie out to cool in expectation of having the pilot and Ernie Simon drop in for lunch. An ermine chanced along, took a sniff and must have decided warm raisins were to his liking. When Eve reached out for the dessert at noon, a good portion of the pie was missing, and the culprit was slinking away with a sagging stomach.

On March 6, 1958 Arrowhead Electric Co-op's power line on the Gunflint Trail was energized.

At Gunflint, as soon as we were hooked in, we ran

down to the lodge and turned on everything at once — the refrigerator, dishwasher, deep freeze, and all the lights — to fully savor the joy of not having to turn off one appliance to turn on another. We hurried to the door and listened almost in disbelief to the silence of the woods. Electricity was no longer accompanied by the throb of our generating plant unconsciously conveying to me its feelings of contentment with a light load or staggering under an overload. It seemed to me a part of my being was gone.

Petra Boostrom hauled out all her unused appliances, which she had stored in the inner recesses of the house. She plugged in the toaster, waffle iron and electric scissors. The scissors, she said, cut carpet rags like a whiz.

The Schlieps plugged in their French frier. Then as Lavern plugged in her iron at the same time, she felt an involuntary hesitation. She forgot for an instant that this light plant would not shudder under the load; it would not be necessary to disconnect the iron at the first dimming of the lights.

I drove down to Mother Bunn's on Hungry Jack and sat before the fireplace in the living room. We looked out the picture window and watched the nuthatches trying to snitch a bit of suet before a squirrel made off with a large chunk. As we were treated to tea and angel food cake, Mother Bunn pulled her iron out of a box. It had been moved so long ago and stored so long that she could not find its cord.

Walter had exchanged the 32-volt bulbs in the house for 110. He curled up on the couch for his first evening of reading his newly-acquired detective stories. He flipped on the light, and it went "ppft" — the one bulb he forgot to change. During our conversation, he suddenly and excitedly exclaimed, "Listen to that water pump in the basement." Instead of struggling for every revolution, it was easily whizzing over. Walter said he looked at the meter each morning with wonder. He felt it should register as rapidly as the light plant had gulped gasoline.

The dream that so many people had worked toward for so long had finally come to pass — Electricity on the Gunflint.

Plumbing

As long as no one on the Trail had modern conveniences — running water and inside plumbing — we were all on a par. The incoming guests graciously accepted the accommodations we had to offer. Then one of our neighbors changed all that.

Dr. Remple owned and operated Northwoods Lodge on Poplar Lake, and he was also the doctor for the CCC (Civilian Conservation Corps) camps. Those camps were built with showers and all the conveniences of city life. As with many government projects there was untold waste. Their dumps contained water pipes of all sizes and lengths; anything that was left over or didn't fit was discarded. Dr. Remple retrieved odd pieces of pipes and stored them at his place. In time he produced running water and inside toilet in one of his cabins. It seemed to make no difference that the pipes were 1½-inch reduced to ½-inch and back to ¾-inch — it worked. And the doctor had the only modern cabin on the Gunflint Trail. We all squirmed.

Doctor Remple's modern cabin with running water intrigued me. The romance, of carrying two pails of water at a time up the long hill to my cabin in the winter, had long since passed.

I discussed the situation with Bill and decided not to take winter guests. I wanted to install a water system, which entailed digging a ditch from the well in front of the lodge, across the road and into the basement of our cabin.

*Hauling Water with a
Shoulder Yoke*

Fortunately we started our dig from the well where, unbeknown to us, there was an overburden of clay intermingled with rocks four feet deep. As we reached the top of the hill the clay petered out and there we found hardpan — a conglomerate of tiny crushed rocks and soil so compacted that a pick slammed into it bounced back as if rejected by an electric shock. When the hardpan was blasted with a carefully-placed stick of dynamite, the conglomerate would rise like the molten innards of a volcano only to drop back in the hole as solid as before.

A ditch needs to be only four feet deep, for accumulating snow forms insulation, which keeps the frost from penetrating more than a couple of feet. But under a road or where the snow is tramped on, the line must go deeper. Our water line passed through an insulated wooden conduit five feet under the road.

After the line was installed and a pump set up in the partially dug basement, lo and behold, we had water in our home. I installed a biffy in one corner, which in my eyes was like a glorified throne that remained unhidden. It was a week before I could bring myself to hide it with a partition.

Alas one cold New Year's day the water ceased to run. I tried to thaw it with every concoction I could think of. The pipe did not break but apparently filled with a slushy hoar frost. It didn't thaw out until mid-June.

We went back to hauling water from the lake and tucking our "privy pads for particular people" under our arms to take to the outhouse. I had scrounged a leftover piece of carpet matting from Mother Kerfoot and cut individual U-shaped pads to place around the frost-covered hole at the outhouse. We hung the pads behind the stove, so they would be warm when needed. Although we always returned with a waffle weave imprint on our behinds, that was preferable to a snowy, frost-covered seat.

We hauled water in winter for our occasional baths. We heated pails and pails of water on the cook stove to fill the washtub placed in the middle of the kitchen. The kitchen got all steamy, and the windows dripped, later forming icy etchings. By lowering our torsos into the tub and letting our feet hang over the side, we could undergo a semblance of an all wet bath.

On wash day we followed the same water heating process. We used a gasoline-operated washing machine which thumped and groaned through every cycle. The clothes taken from the washer were run through the hand wringer. It was a hand-numbing operation hanging them on the line outside to freeze dry. After a day of hanging stiff at odd angles in sub-zero temperatures, the clothes were brought back to the house and strung up on cords for their final drying. As they thawed, they looked like headless ghosts in mid-air that finally died and went limp.

We postponed the inevitable as long as possible, but the time finally came when, to stay competitive, we had to modernize our cabins.

Friends of ours in St. Paul knew the manager of the plumbing department at Montgomery Wards. They arranged an appointment for me. At that time the mail order section of the store would draw up blueprints and make a complete plumbing layout, listing all the equipment needed. Armed with a sketch of the locations of the cabins and their distances from the well, I met this kindly gentleman and explained my needs to him.

He looked at me with a quizzical gleam in his eye and casually asked, "Who is going to install this system for you?"

Feeling my world of modernization was in jeopardy, I lied, "I have a brother who is a plumber."

He glanced at me with a knowing smile and asked for my sketch. After studying it and asking a few pertinent questions he remarked, "Without question I think this is the worst outline we have ever seen." I was momentarily crushed until he added, "I think we can help you, though."

In time several pages of detailed blueprints arrived. Then came a truckload of water pipes of assorted sizes, sewer pipes and auxiliary pieces for a complete installation. This was accompanied by a full complement of tools. There was a pipe threader with a full set of dies, pipe cutter, a pipe vise, lead for sewer joints along with a tamp bar, a coil of oakum and a can of pipe sealer. When everything was unloaded, the scene was mind-boggling. A fleeting doubt passed through my mind. But the layout was so complete, the details so explicit, that I felt I couldn't miss even though the tools all looked foreign to me.

When I started our installations, Bill was either cutting wood or off to a political meeting. Anyway he had claustrophobia about crawling under a cabin. Since I installed the water line from underneath the cabins, a few pipes did not follow the custom of hot water on the left and cold on the right. The perspective from underneath seemed correct. But when I crawled out from under the cabin and looked at it from the top, I found that some were reversed. Oh well. So be it. We had water in our cabins.

In the spring we hand dug holes for the septic tanks.

We invariably came upon a large boulder, usually halfway down. The boulders had to be pried loose, lifted with long poles and raised inch by inch by inserting rocks underneath. The first time Bill and I dropped a big septic tank in a six-foot hole and covered it, we were amazed to find it had popped up two or three feet above ground by the next morning. We had to dig it out again and pull it free of the hole. Dirt as well as ground water had sifted in along the sides. We painfully learned to fill the tank with water the moment it is dropped into the hole. Slowly and painstakingly the plumbing was completed.

Since the lodge was built on a slope with the front on pilings, there was a natural space underneath for a shower. I installed a jerry rig shower with refreshing cold water only, but it was not always available for the use of our guests. Our calf Ferdinand claimed it as his own and a guest arriving in a robe would often be greeted by him, declaring with his stance that he was first.

We acquired Ferdinand to nibble off the tall grass which grew with the impetus of a hay field once we cleared the underbrush. All around the lodge and cabins the tall grass thrived, harboring swarms of mosquitoes and blackflies. We tried cutting it with a scythe — the ground was too rocky to mow — but with our ineptness the grass popped up again after every swath.

I suggested to Bill we get a nanny goat. It could keep the grass short as well as supply us with rich milk. He said, "Goats smell." In the heat of our argument the farmer who sold Mother the pig stopped in. The next time by he dropped off a small calf which he said would do the job. We took it to our "pasture" but it would not eat the grass. It just looked at us. Consequently we had to buy buckets of milk powder to mix with water and supply his nourishment.

The calf grew, but so did the grass. That summer there seemed to be just one place where Ferdinand felt cool and comfortable: under the lodge on the cement floor of the shower.

The Kerfeet Three

Bruce Todd, Pat Mariona and Sharon Lane were born at three-year intervals, 1938, 1942 and 1945. It is always smart for resorters to have babies in winter. Bruce was born in December, but Pat defied all regulations by investigating this world in June. Sharon made her debut in February. With these births, having previously lost a baby, I went to Duluth 10 days early and sat it out in a hotel, awaiting the pleasure of their highnesses.

Bruce was born the year of the deep snow. A month after I came home to Gunflint with the baby,

Netowance Plummer, left, and Mary Cook

Mrs. Plummer and Mrs. Cook snowshoed over to see the new boy. They carefully brushed their moccasins before they came in. They peeked at the baby in his bassinet, smiled and chatted with each other in Chippewa, looked at me approvingly and departed.

Butchie took a special liking to Bruce and one day she brought over a tick-a-noggin. Our guests sent us a deluge of baby blankets, caps, mittens, sweaters and buntings as gifts on Bruce's birth. Butchie showed me how to arrange the blankets, lay the baby on the backboard, fold the blankets around his legs and arms,

Baby Bruce Laced in his Tick-A-Noggin with Mother

tuck a blanket over the top and lace him in. Bruce loved the warmth and snugness of this cocoon. He was amply protected from evil spirits by the adorning Indian charms which hung on each side of the protective head bar. They were circular in shape with the center woven to resemble a spider web. Indian tick-a-noggins were equipped with a tump line; I added pack straps to mine, which I found more convenient. When I carried Bruce on my back while snowshoeing, he would invariably fall asleep, being rocked by the rhythm of my steps.

115

When Bruce was about two, Bill and I had an opportunity to drive to The Pas, Manitoba and take the train to Churchill. It was our first vacation. I had never left the baby with anyone, but Butchie said she would take care of him. The day before we left Butchie came over for instructions. I lined up the cans of baby food so Bruce would have a balanced diet. I told her how to smack him on his back in case he got something caught in his throat. I couldn't leave written instructions, since Butchie couldn't read, but I showed her how to use the phone in case she needed help. She sat there silently with the stoicism of a sphinx. After all my warnings she had only one comment, "Baby no get anything in his mouth. I keep house clean."

On our return two weeks later, Bruce hid behind Butchie wondering who these strangers were. The house was spotless and the baby immaculate. The baby food was neatly lined up on a shelf in two separate compartments. One contained the full supply of beets, carrots, spinach and beans. The other compartment, almost depleted, had a few cans of applesauce, fruit and a supply of pablum.

Indicating the vegetables, I asked, "Butchie, why didn't you use these cans?"

She answered, "Baby no like."

Pat, born in mid-June, was slow in gaining strength after her arrival. The pediatrician suggested she stay in the hospital an extra week where she could receive an ample supply of mother's milk. (I was of little help.) Mothers stayed in the hospital for 10 days after births then, so there were mothers available to supply milk. I returned to the lodge. In two weeks a doctor, Elizabeth Bagley, and nurse Marion Smith, friends of mine, delivered the tiny, but now stronger, baby to Gunflint.

Sharon arrived in February, just missing Valentines Day, with ringlets of golden hair. She declared her independence at an early age.

116

Bill, Me and the Kerfeet Three

Children in a Remote Wilderness

Raising a family in the remote woods was somewhat like raising a family on a distant ranch, for there was a minimum of contact with other children. At the American Plan resort we operated, the clientele was mostly adults. The children acquired adults' vocabularies — both good and bad. Our youngsters contracted no children's diseases and were free from colds.

On the other hand they did not develop resistance to measles, mumps and such afflictions. When they first started public schools, they were comparable to the Indians who, when first exposed to the white man's diseases, went down like ten pins.

In retrospect I have kaleidoscopic flashes of endless

117

diapers to be washed, babies to be fed and bathed, guests to be cared for, motors to be repaired and the overloaded light plant to be cajoled into carrying a few more watts.

There was a whole series of incidents like those that face many mothers in the art of raising a family.

When Bruce was in the high chair I hurriedly gave him a dish of oatmeal and placed him in an adjoining room off the kitchen. When I had a chance to return I found him with a gleeful grin, for he had turned the entire contents upside down over his head.

After Bruce learned to walk, Butchie watched out the window as he carried a kitten in his arms to the outhouse and returned empty-handed. Aggie called me to tell me of the incident. I questioned Bruce, and he professed a total lack of knowledge of the whereabouts of the kitten. I sallied toward the biffy. As I opened the door I heard a plaintive cry from the bottom of the toilet pit. We had to build a miniature ladder to lower into the hole for the kitten's escape route. Much persuasion was needed to get the kitten to climb out of the excrement into which it had been dropped. Aggie watched from the window as the kitten appeared from its confines, shaking its feet with each step.

When Pat was just able to toddle around she chanced into the dining room and was immediately picked up by Eddie Fisher, one of our long-time fisherman guests. He satisfied her apparent hunger by holding her on his lap while he fed her, bit by bit, the entire contents of his raisin pie.

It was a hard and fast rule that no youngster could go on the dock without a life jacket. When Pat forgot this ruling, she was grounded for a week and she stood on shore dejectedly watching others paddling in the water.

When Sharon arrived, a pecking order was established. Pat was excited over her new sister, watched over her and kept her out of trouble. She also adored her brother who, in her eyes, could do no wrong.

Sharon rebelled against the menial tasks which everyone had to share, but she often offered bits of sage advice. One spring day we found our basement flooded with the runoff of melting snow. Bruce was in the basement scooping up pails of water. I had a rope attached to the pail, and I pulled it up through the root cellar hole in the floor and carried it a dozen steps to dump in the kitchen sink. Sharon watched me with interest, and then asked, "Why don't you pour it down the toilet?" Since this eliminated the steps, I adopted this four-year-old's suggestion.

When it came time for Bruce to start school, the options were not great. We could find a family in Grand Marais to board him during the week, close the northwoods home and move out, or teach him an accredited course at home. I chose the latter, and I taught Bruce for three years. He complained when Pat scribbled on his school papers and Sharon crawled around trying to eat the crayons. We kept a schedule that never altered, even though a spelling lesson was sometimes heard from under the truck where I was making a repair, and Bruce sat on the running board answering my challenges.

I used the Calvert School's correspondence course, whose lessons are challenging and informative. They taught me some lessons too — one question asked of the student was, "What if you were black?" I thought, "What if my son's skin were black. What opportunities would be curtailed? What restrictions would be placed on his activities? How would he be accepted in a largely white man's world?" When we think in those terms the differences we find in other peoples become acceptable.

In a parent's eyes the first child often seems to be especially gifted. They walk and talk earlier and are more astute than other youngsters of comparable age. I started teaching Bruce in the fall when he was still five. I saw little progress, so I wrote the Calvert School to ask what I was doing wrong. I assumed it was my teaching methods and not Burce's inability to absorb what was presented to him. I received a very nice letter in return which read something like this: "My dear Mrs. Kerfoot; We would suggest that you wait and try again at several month intervals. When your son reaches an age capable of absorbing the material you will be aware of the fact."

When Bruce was a little past six, the learning process "took." I taught each of our children in turn some longer than others as conditions gradually changed.

As long as I was teaching Bruce, I thought it an opportunity to teach Butchie to read and write. She came across the lake each day for lessons. Although she made some progress, the driving force was missing. The readers discussed farms, farm animals, people in cities and other nationalities. If the subject matter were mink and otter, beaver, deer and moose or the winds, the seasons and the restless waters, reading may have stimulated her interest.

Besides why should Butchie learn to write when no other member of her family could read a note or write one in return? She did learn to sign her name and read a few essential words found in a small town.

When Bruce was about 12 he boarded with Andy and Hildur Hedstrom on Maple Hill. He attended the Maple Hill School, where he had his first close contact with other children his age. Non-acceptance was mutual, and each weekend he took out his frustrations on his sisters. Eventually Pat joined Bruce in school and also boarded with the Hedstrom family.

Then I had an opportunity to acquire a home on Maple Hill just six miles north of Grand Marais and a couple of miles west of the Gunflint Trail. I could tether the dogs there without annoying the neighbors, and the home was on a school bus route. Although the boarding homes were with the finest people, by living at Maple Hill during the winter months, I could have the children home with me. They still boarded during the week in the spring and fall, and the school bus came up the Trail on weekends, as an accommodation to resort operators.

By this time Bill had become so involved in politics, his true love, that he seldom returned home and finally not at all. We permanently parted when Bruce was in high school.

Finally the children were each sent off to college. Bruce to the hotel school at Cornell at Ithaca, New York; Pat to LaCrosse, Wisconsin; and Sharon to St. Olaf, at Northfield, Minnesota. While the girls were going to college, my lodge staffs were well-picked, for the applicants they screened proved to be the best.

Bruce worked at an eastern hotel one summer as part of his program. He joined ROTC and then after college served two years in the army. Then he returned home and gradually worked into the Gunflint Lodge business, finally taking it over.

Pat taught in Washington, fell in love and married a biology teacher. After teaching in Kodiak, Alaska for a few years, they started a fly-in resort on Wein Lake within sight of the Alaskan range and Mt. McKinley.

Sharon ended up in California, attended UCLA to obtain paralegal training, married a lawyer and works with her husband in his law firm. Although they were raised in the woods, they all adapted well to the challenges of competitive living.

CHAPTER 5

"CRISES"

Surrounded by Forest Fires

THE Civilian Conservation Corps was set up during the depression to create employment for young men in their upper teens. There were four or five camps on the Trail, including one for veterans. Each camp was complete with large bunkhouses, mess halls, modern showers with latrine facilities, trucks and machinery for sizable work projects. The camps were operated by army lieutenants, and all the men were kept at the camps when not working. They planted trees in burned or logged-over areas, fought the blister rust that was affecting the white pines and built a 10-mile telephone line to Sea Gull Lake. They fought forest fires and cut trails: the Rib Lake tote road and the Kekakabic and Winchell Lake fire trails.

Many of the CCC participants had never been outside a city, and this camp life had a lasting effect on them. Living in the woods where they had to be dependent on each other gave them new values and a new outlook for their lives. The CCC men worked arduously during the 1936 fires; without their manpower thousands of acres of forest would have been consumed.

After the spring breakup in the summer of 1936, the woods were drier than usual. By August the fire danger to the forest was critical. Every morning we would gaze skyward searching for a semblance of a cloud. But the sun rose and continued to pour out its heat as summer progressed. We sought places to cool off: the shade, the water or even the root cellar. Then it happened.

That morning when Abie Cook came across the lake, we stopped to talk at the dock house. Abie pointed to a slight curl of smoke halfway down the lake and back in the hills. Surveyors were working in that area, and a careless flick from a pipe or cigarette probably started the fire. We notified the Forest Service, but they could do nothing because it was on the Canadian side. The Canadian Forestry were not interested. They had fire troubles nearer farms and towns where many people's lives and investments were in jeopardy. These faraway woods were at the bottom of the priority list.

The fire smoldered and slowly gained momentum. The wind toyed with it, teasing it first one way and then another. It progressed steadily toward the Granite River, then changed directions as a west wind drove it the opposite way. As it grew, it created a backdraft that even carried it against the wind, albeit more slowly. Finally after about a week, there was a breakthrough.

Harvey   Bishop

Forest Fire Blazing

worked for the Canadian Forestry and lived on North Lake. He was released along with a limited amount of equipment to fight the "Gunflint" fire. At the same time the local people joined forces with some of the CCC men, and a little equipment from the American side was made available.

Walter Plummer, who knew the country well, laid out a line. It went from one small lake to another, and finally followed a trail (that once existed from a logging camp situated on the last pond) back to Gunflint Lake. The fire was held in abeyance for a while, for Harvey and Walter knew how to dispel men to the best advantage. And they also knew how to fight forest fires. But in spite of this effort, the ultimate outcome was dependent on the whims of the wind and the chances of rain.

In fire fighting a canoe was often placed at the end of a hose line between ponds, where water was not obtainable. The canoe was used as a reservoir, and by synchronizing pumps, water could be relayed where needed.

At about this time other fires developed in our area. Great clouds of smoke were rolling from a large fire, which became known as the Frost Lake fire. Another large fire suddenly sprang up in the Quetico. Surprisingly, with these fires almost surrounding us, we received very little smoke. The smoke conditions, of course, were controlled by the wind.

There were many lakes between the fires and our lodge, acting as safety barriers for us. Since we had a large proportion of deciduous trees interspersed with the pine, we had little worry of the fire "topping." The fire did however pick up pieces of flaming birch bark. And the self-created draft sent these torches aloft to land and start other fires.

By 1936 more resorts and summer homes were established along the Trail. Some people panicked during the fires while others stayed calm. Harry Anderson, owner of Tuscarora Lodge on Round Lake, packed up most of his personal belongings and left for Grand Marais. On Gunflint Lake, the Morriseys, a family who had a summer home a mile from Gunflint Lodge, left for the Twin Cities with their belongings. I was alone to make the decisions, for Bill had developed a bad case of ulcers and jaundice and was in a Duluth hospital.

All of the resorters were concerned about their guests, whose safety was paramount. We all had to decide whether to hold our people or let them drive down the Trail. They could be caught in a traffic jam, where there were no nearby lakes for a safety buffer. Since we were at the end of the telephone service, we felt obliged to notify our neighbors of the status of the fires.

The Merrys, former guests of ours, had a home on their 120 acres which adjoined our 100-acre holdings. Ray Merry agreed with me that we would be much safer at Gunflint Lake (which is a mile wide and eight miles long) than caught on a narrow winding road with the possibility of smoke obliterating all visibility. We planned together to combine our boat fleets for the protection of his family and our guests if it were necessary to go out on the lake.

I called Petra Boostrom. They had guests and were getting quite a bit of smoke. Her reaction was to take it cool. Charlie had been out fighting fires for the past several weeks because he was familiar with the country. She felt there was no immediate danger.

Because of Gunflint Lake's depth and our dock facilities, we became a staging and dispersal point. Planes flew in and out every 15-20 minutes from dawn to dusk.

The wind changed. The fire on Gunflint burned the north ridges and headed for the Granite River. The far side of the river was mostly jack pine, which burns with a hot

125

fire. If it continued in that direction, the fire could threaten Sea Gull Resort.

On Magnetic Bay the Plummers moved their belongings down on their dock, for the fire was on the high hills behind them. The wind changed again and the fire swept along to the northeast. The State Forestry, headed by Pat Bayle (my friend Gene's uncle) brought in fire fighting equipment. They went to North Lake to protect the forestry cabin located on a point near the narrows leading into North Lake proper.

Permission was finally granted for Americans to fight the fire along the border on the Canadian side. The bureaucratic decision was slow in coming, for it was based, not on how best to stop the fire, but rather on who was going to pay for the men, transportation and food involved. Should Canada foot the bill for American crews and equipment working on their soil? Or should it be the Americans who pay to prevent the fire from jumping and destroying property and timber on the American side? An agreement was reached that a corridor of two-and-one-half miles on each side of the border would be available permanently to fire fighting crews from each government. This agreement opened the door for an intelligent way to fight fires along the Minnesota-Ontario border.

Next, a southwest wind took the fire, by leaps and bounds, toward Northern Light Lake. Then the wind suddenly changed again and picked up force, moving the fire toward Little Gunflint and Little North Lakes.

As Pat Bayle said, "It came through like a thundering express." His pumps and hoses were directed at the forestry cabin and surrounding buildings in an effort to soak down the area. As the fire approached the men moved their equipment to a raft, still directing water on buildings and pulling clear of the oncoming inferno. When the smoke cleared, the forestry building was left standing intact, but the nearby boat house with its outpost supplies as well as the outhouse had vanished.

In the meantime a group of CCC men were brought in to maintain a fire line along the North-South Lake portage. A gust of wind carried some flaming embers across to the heavily-forested ridge between North and South Lakes. Pat Bayle had anticipated this. He had set up a line on the north side of the ridge and directed the leaders of the CCC crew to set up a line on the ridge's south side. They moved in, and it looked as if the fire could be stopped cold. But at noon the CCC leader told the men to stop for lunch. They shut down the pumps and went back to the portage to eat. The fire was like a wild beast waiting for a way to escape. It jumped the unguarded line, and Pat Bayle had to withdraw his handful of men.

The ridge acted like a chimney fire completely out of control creating a draft from both sides. The fire burned with such fury that night that one could read a paper by its light in the middle of Gunflint Lake eight miles away.

A new fire line was established near Rose Lake, and this is where the fire ended. A combination of the men on the new line, a reversal of the wind and finally a little rain left the fire a harmless and spent beast.

The rains came. The fires subsided and left the earth to renew itself. The landscape was changed — the forested ridge was now bare. Nary a stubble was left on the ridge, or along either shore of the channel from Gunflint to North Lake.

World War II

During World War II there were all types of rationing. Because it was a 50-mile drive to town — our nearest source of supplies — the gasoline shortage was one of our most drastic restrictions.

Each resort had their own truck and made weekly trips to town over these roads for mail and supplies. During these years flat tires were frequently changed en route as rocks and sharp stones took their toll. Improvising was a way of life. We used a heavy strip of birch bark as a tire boot. Supported a broken spring with a chunk of birch wood. Laced a leather strap together to replace a fan belt. We used hay wire to tie together anything that broke. And added water to an almost-empty gas tank to lift the level higher and save a couple miles of walking.

Border Regulations

Canada maintained a number of prisoner of war camps during the war, and several men had escaped from them. On a July day in 1943, the Canadian-Minnesota boundary was ordered closed to all Canadians except those who had passports and went through a regular point of entry. Although our traffic, remote as we were, consisted of only a handful of Canadian Indians coming across the lake for supplies, mail and employment as guides, this sweeping regulation applied to our border. But Gunflint Lake is international water, so the Indians were allowed to come across the lake as long as they didn't step on our dock or on U.S. soil. The regulations did not affect American citizens.

Our local situation became ludicrous. Our Canadian friends who worked as guides for us, came across the lake and pulled their boats up to our dock without stepping on shore. We packed the lunches and cooking utensils and loaded the guests into our boats. Then the guides stepped from their boats into our boats, took our parties out for the day and had a noon cookup on the Canadian shore. On their return the guides stepped back into their own boats and went back home across the lake. We cleaned the lunch boxes and prepared them for the next day. And we iced and packed the fish — tasks usually handled by the guides.

The Indians relished a perverse satisfaction in our being called on to provide "dock service." We served them beer, pop, candy, cigarettes and even gave them haircuts in their boats. In spite of this ridiculous aspect of the curtailment it lasted until the next spring.

One day during this time Charlie Cook came to tell us there was a strange human track on the old railroad right-of-way. A canoe left on one side of the Magnetic narrows had been moved over to the opposite shore. We notified the Border Patrol. It turned out that a pilot had escaped from a prisoner camp. He obviously had an accomplice on this side who knew the terrain, for the pilot had been met and whisked away, making an effective escape without being apprehended.

Most of our guests during the war were professional people taking a short respite from the long, long hours of their war efforts. Others were recovering from the loss of a son. In effect we became an R and R, a rest and recreation area.

During the early winter of 1943 two lads John Bollenbacker and Walter Rietz came to the lodge and followed Bill on an overnight to his trapline. They walked the fire trail that extended from the Gunflint Trail to George Lake. While in there they spent a few days building a small trapping shack for Bill to use.

John Bollenbacker, who went into the service after helping build the trappers shack, sent us a verse written by Vern Helmen.

Nostalgia

Let me return to the Northland
To the deer and the streams and the larch.
To that shack beside the Gunflint
For haven at the end of this march.
Where a man's success is measured in sweat
His pay a happy life.
There let me live and build and thrive
Forgetting these years of strife.
A venison steak and wild rice
Not caviar and paste.
A balsam bed and cedar fire
Fresh air enough to waste.
Tooth-chilling water from out of the North
Day slipping quietly away.
The eerie shriek of a loon at night
I want to return and stay.

The Wilderness Express, Our Lifeline

With rationing curtailing travel, we turned for help to Don Brazell. In April 1933 Don had started making weekly trips from Grand Marais to all the resorts on the Trail as a beer service. The resort operators sighed with relief. No longer must they travel the narrow, hilly, twisty road for every needed item. Incoming guests had been "trained" to stop and pick up the mail, but now this service was augmented by Don as a personal friendly gesture. Over the years Don became a vital link who made it possible for the resorts to operate successfully.

In between runs he graciously shopped for us and picked up innumerable small items from personal packages to a spool of thread or a package of bandages. His arrival was like the stagecoach coming. All the neighbors came from across the lake to socialize or to pick up an item Don might have for them.

Don became authorized to carry the mail officially on a Star Route, after the necessary surveys were made and forms filled out. Our mail service ballooned to twice a week in summer and once a week in winter.

In 1943 Bill Kerfoot, Russell Blankenburg and several others made a number of trips to St. Paul to meet the Railroad and Warehouse Commission. Their aim was to negotiate a license for Don Brazell to carry passengers non-stop from Duluth to the Gunflint Trail. At that time there was train travel from Chicago, Minneapolis-St. Paul, and intermediate points to Duluth, but the Greyhound bus schedule was not compatible — a day's layover in Duluth was required for guests going in either direction. And it meant each resort making a trip to town to pick up their guests, which was especially difficult with tight gas rationing.

Don Brazell's Freight Truck and Neighbors

The meetings were successful, and a permit was granted for the duration of the war.

So Don bought two buses. One bus came up from Duluth to End of the Trail Lodge as the other bus went down. They were named the "Wilderness Express," but a more accurate description would be the lifeline of the Gunflint Trail. Don drove in all the side roads directly to the resorts. Those who rode the Wilderness Express recall with nostalgia the friendly contacts and repartee between passengers as they exchanged tales of their adventures.

In 1945 at the end of the war, Bill and I were not taking winter guests. We received a phone call from a girl in Duluth who wanted to come to the woods for a week or two. I told her we weren't taking guests at this time. We were trying to dig the ditch to get water to the cabin, and I just didn't have time to cook and cater to guests. She replied that she had just returned home from serving overseas with the Red Cross. She had dreamed of getting to the peacefulness of the woods. As a clincher, she added she would help where she could and she would not require special attention. I acquiesced.

I turned from the phone and Bill said, "I thought you weren't going to take guests."

I answered, "She just returned from the war and wants a breather." So Janet Hanson came to Gunflint.

After Janet had been with us a couple of weeks, I received a call from Dad who was in Florida for the winter with Mother. While en route to Florida with Dad, she had suffered a severe stroke from which there was no hope of recovery. Dad wanted me to come to Florida to help make future plans.

I was in a bind. We had deer hunters coming to the lodge in another two weeks, who would need me to cook. Then there were Bill and the children to consider. Janet

Janet Hanson, the First Outfitters

volunteered to stay. She would take care of the family and cook for the hunters their first day. By then I would return. In fact we passed each other — as she was leaving Gunflint, I was returning from Florida.

Janet returned over the holidays with friends from southern Illinois where she was teaching. We agreed she should come the next summer and work at the front desk. Janet was aggressive and outgoing. She had degrees in physical education from the University of Minnesota and Columbia.

Her ultimate desire was to operate a canoe outfitting business. We were operating a small canoe business with a dozen canoes and equipment for complete outfitting. With this as a nucleus we entered into a partnership that lasted 25 years. For 20 years Janet and I had a booth at the winter sport shows in Milwaukee, Chicago and Minneapolis.

She started the operation in an 8x10 converted tool shed. A year or so later she moved it to a remodeled garage and finally into a large outfitters building newly-constructed for the expanding business. The business grew from her single Jeep and a dozen canoes to a hundred canoes, a fleet of vans, a sizable crew and all the dehydrated foods and equipment necessary for a successful outfitting operation.

Eventually Janet started a canoe business of her own further up the Trail.

In early spring there was always a deluge of applications from college students looking for summer work. Most applicants stated what work they would consider. They usually emphasized how much they liked to fish, swim and canoe. It was an interesting contrast when in 1952 we received an application from Eleanor Matsis. She stated she would like employment for the summer and would work wherever needed. She was hired as a dishwasher when electric dishwashers were unknown.

Mat, as she was called, was a New Englander, a graduate of Smith College and a math teacher. She soon put her mechanical and numerical talents to good use. She organized and disposed of her dishwashing chores with dispatch and then searched for more challenging jobs. Mat called Gunflint her home for the next 17 years, working year-round for the first ten. Then she drove the Trail each day to teach in Grand Marais in winter and worked at the lodge in summer. She eventually made Minneapolis her home, where she pursued her teaching career.

The Lodge Becomes a Towering Flame

Before daylight on a June morning in 1953 I was awakened by the persistent yowling of Pat's cat outside my window. I smelled smoke — lots of smoke. The lodge building was on fire. Since fire protection in the woods was almost nil, fire was a hazard we always watched for and guarded against.

Lobby Interior, Before the Fire

The family and help were roused. Bill awakened the guests and ran to shut off the oil tanks and electricity. The fire had started in the farthest corner of the lounge. I opened the front door a crack to see if I could crawl along the floor and retrieve the mailing list, the records, or the movies of dog team trips. The open door gave the flames more oxygen, and the fire accelerated. I could not enter.

Janet first notified the Forest Service and then started moving outfitting equipment out of the converted garage. We formed bucket brigades to save adjacent buildings. At that early hour there was no wind, so the flames towered high and straight.

By six o'clock the lodge was all gone. Two stark stone fireplaces and the twisted ruins of stoves, sinks and pipes smoldered in the ruins.

The furniture, made from the surrounding woods, caused the fire to burn very hot. Everything had vanished: the mounted moose and deer heads denoting my first hunt, the 100-year-old grandfather clock given to me as the oldest granddaughter, books, records, reservations and movies. A safe containing some now-scorched papers sat upright where the office had been. The slightly smoked contents of a freezer were intact; the freezer still sat where there had been a back porch. All the trees in front of the lodge had burned too. Joe Blackjack planted these, and they had grown tall and straight.

The fire was a double misfortune. A young man staying overnight at our canoe camp sought more comfort. In the middle of the night he sauntered up to the lodge, entered the building and settled himself in an overstuffed easy chair. He apparently went to sleep while smoking a cigarette. As the chair smoldered it gave off lethal fumes and finally burst into flame consuming him.

The roused guests had gathered at a respectful distance to watch the roaring flames which were confined to the one building. After the fire was out, we sent the guests back to their cabins. We told them we would notify them shortly as to what actions we would take.

The crew stood around in a tight huddle, certain their jobs had evaporated. I turned to them and said, "Move! Clear my living room, use my kitchen; get some boards and put them across two sawhorses, and find some long benches for the guests to sit on." We were lucky, in a way, for we had a root cellar full of canned goods and vegetables, and we had a separate storeroom where we kept all the dry goods.

Word of the catastrophe had somehow spread as quickly as a lapping wave touching shore. Our loyal neighbors immediately brought dishes, pots and pans, silver and china in whatever quantities they could spare. Within a couple of hours my cabin was converted into a kitchen, pantry and dining room where we could seat and serve our guests in two shifts.

A special truck came up from town bringing bread, eggs, milk and perishables. Breakfast was served by nine. It all looked workable, so the guests stayed. And no one checked out. As they all gathered around one table a camaraderie developed among them. The candy, pop, cigarettes and cigars were piled in a corner with a cigar box where people placed their money and made their own change; the code of honor never faltered.

Re-adaptation, Rebuilding

While a group of us sat looking at the smoldering ruins wondering what move to make, a neighbor Pearl Brown approached me. She had a cabin two miles down the shore and was retired from running a tavern catering to families. She unobtrusively slipped a piece of paper into my hand with the remark, "You can't solve it by sitting and grieving." It was a check for $1000, a silent understanding of a loan for a new start.

After the Fire, Pearl Brown on far left

I jumped in the car and drove 25 miles down the Trail to talk to Charlie Boostrom. He and Petra had recently sold their lodge to the Schlieps. Charlie was semi-retired, only building log cabins for his neighbors and starting a new stone home for himself and Petra.

I told him of my catastrophe, my need for a deep foundation that would not heave each spring and settle in midsummer, and my need of his help. He looked at me with a smile. He said he could help get the foundation in, but he couldn't promise to do the entire building. I asked him when he could start. He answered, "Tomorrow." He called Ed Thoreson, a contractor in Grand Marais, who said he would come immediately and start excavating for the walls.

I hurried back up the Trail to find the contractor who was rebuilding the road from Loon Lake to the Tuscarora junction. He sent in his big equipment and cleaned up the mess. Later his superintendent gave us a lift when we needed to cart away boulders encountered during excavation.

Bill and I sketched the shape and location of the new lodge on a piece of wrapping paper. Charlie said that was all he needed. His crew consisted of himself, his pal Chris Brotan and Frank Horak who had lost one arm in a sawing accident. These old timers took pride in their work and their abilities. As the new foundation took shape neighbors, summer residents and guests would stop to visit, saw a board, pound a nail or give hours or days of their time and energy. In reality building the lodge became a community affair.

After the foundation was finished, Charlie decided to stay on and see the project completed. I wanted to get the basic plumbing in before the subfloor was laid to avoid working in a crawl space under the building. Mat helped me with the project while Bill was working on other facets. The hours necessary to complete the plumbing were of no small consequence. Even as Charlie and his crew started laying the subfloor, and we were still installing the plumbing, we bobbed up between the floor stringers to see if we could finish before we were covered. We just made it.

On the morning of June 28, 1953, there had been a smoldering ruin. Two months later there arose a new lodge. During the interim, the building surge was intermingled

Steve Leonard Photo

Charlie Boostrom

with caring for guests and their activities. On August 25 we moved into the completed building — in reality only a shell with exposed studding and a subfloor, but it was more spacious than my log house. The guests set cans of wild flowers around on the open studdings, and we celebrated this landmark accomplishment.

The new lodge was T-shaped and had log siding. The lobby and dining room consisted of a 90-foot span with large picture windows overlooking the lake. The office, kitchen and staff dining room comprised the balance of the lodge. We purchased a smattering of California redwood furniture for the lobby, but we still used planks, sawhorses and benches in the dining room for the balance of the season.

In midsummer Mat asked if she could stay on and work over the winter for her room and board to experience a winter in the north woods. We agreed, but little did she dream of the work that was going to be involved.

New Lodge, before the Fireplaces were Built

Fire insurance on the lodge was quite inadequate. And it took almost all our savings to complete the structure and buy the oak flooring and aspen paneling that we thought appropriate.

We had on hand a load of oak flooring 1½-inches wide, excluding the tongue and groove. When we laid the first boards end to end along the length of the 60-foot lounge, I had a feeling of trying to stretch a piece of string around the equator.

The proper way to lay a floor is to stand, lean over and nail. That was back-breaking, so we tried working on our knees. No one had informed us about oak: it is not particularly receptive to finishing nails. It is necessary to drill holes first. The nails might be driven in if they are first dipped in oil. After bending a bunch of nails on our first try, then drilling holes which was laboriously slow, we stacked a fistful of nails in a tumbler of oil — our final solution. After driving the nails as far as we could, we drove the boards together by laying a chunk of birch against the flooring and striking it several times with a maul. This

140

drew the boards together into a compact unit.

There were two jovial, chubby ex-sailors Loren Davis and Grady, who had a cabin a quarter-mile down the road. They offered to give us a hand with the flooring for a few days. They started out kneeling, then sitting, then lying on an elbow while pounding nails. And then they came no more.

The children, now 9 - 12 - 15, were put to work when they were home. They were boarding in town this fall, returning home on Friday and leaving Monday morning. Sharon and Pat hauled boards into place while Bruce pounded with a steady rat-a-tat-tat. The lobby seemed to take forever to complete. But the dining room which was half that size did not seem such a task, and the office was a breeze.

That winter we moved to the house on Maple Hill. There was a barn which I converted into a workshop. I thought I should be able to build tables and chairs for the dining room and lounge from native wood, as George Bayle did for Mother when she first enlarged the lodge.

Before attempting to build furniture for the lodge, I scouted the woods for red birch with a diameter of three to four inches for chairs. I finally collected a truckload and hauled it to the "shop." A couple of chairs had survived the fire, since they were in another building for repair. I used one of these for a sample. It really looked quite simple. I carved all the necessary pieces and assembled it. I discovered the legs were not absolutely even and it teetered. When I leaned back in it the joints creaked and stretched. The entire thing was a wobbly mess. In tearful fury I gave it an unrestrained kick and watched it disintegrate at my feet. With over 50 chairs and a dozen tables to be produced, I made a new start.

This time I created an assembly line. First I made all the backs, then all the fronts and finally joined them together. They became one solid piece. The seats and table tops, made out of thick birch boards doweled and glued together, were added last. This phase was not completed until Mat had sanded, buffed and varnished these units nine times. Only then could they become a part of the finished product.

When the first four chairs and a table were completed, we hauled them up to the lodge and placed them in the dining room. What a disillusioning jolt! The effect was of placing a stool in the center of a banquet hall.

It took all winter to complete the furniture. During that time the family absorbed sawdust inside and out and inhaled varnish as various pieces were brought in the house to dry. In the early spring after returning to the lodge, we lined the inside of the building with aspen. The oak floor was sanded with an electric sander rented from a store in town. The building was complete — almost.

A couple of years had passed when Pearl Brown looked at the inside of the lodge with an appraising eye. She said, "It's time for the fireplaces." Again she slipped a check into my hand, for the same amount as her original loan. (I had repaid the first gift.)

Tables and Chairs

Once more I headed for my mentor Charlie Boostrom, 25 miles down the Trail at his home on Clearwater Lake. He was in the midst of building their new stone house. I found him in the basement "laying up a stone wall."

Charlie glanced up without losing a movement in his work, as I sat down and dangled my feet over this cavernous hole. With some trepidation I asked if he would have time to build a couple of fireplaces for me in the fall. There was dead silence as if I had spoken to the rock wall. I waited. Five minutes may have passed but it seemed like an eternity. Finally he said, "After I finish these walls, I think I can spare the time. But first you gather the rocks and have them on hand." I told him I hoped the dining room fireplace would be built from granite. The granite had to be split like severing an upright log with an axe.

I gleefully left to go rock gathering. Charlie had taken time to show me how some granite rocks were conglomerates and would not split, and how others had a grain you could find like in a piece of wood. The two types of granite are analogous to two trees — one with a straight grain that splits easily, and one so twisted and full of knots that it can't be split.

Charlie had an extra stone hammer which he loaned me. It was a heavy long-handled maul with a head of four square corners. The trick was to hit the grain with a mighty belt on the edge of a square corner, cleaving the rock into two parts. There were many granite rocks along our side road, so we thought the loading would be easy. Mat drove the truck while I did the splitting.

Splitting rocks is an art that I was unable to develop. I would slam a rock as Charlie had illustrated and leave just a peck mark instead of a clean cleavage. With a success of one dozen rocks split in a two-mile stretch, I made another trip to Charlie. He agreed to come up and split the rocks if we gathered a pile large enough to complete the fireplace. But we were forewarned they had to be big rocks.

We put two large planks at a slope off the back of the truck. The rocks we were unable to lift we rolled up these boards. After several days of weary labor we told Charlie of our supply. He came up on a weekend and split the entire pile. It was awe-inspiring. We brought in sacks of cement from town and hauled several truckloads of light gravel which we screened.

Charlie came to build the first fireplace. In retrospect that week is a complete blur. The conversation consisted of four words: "More mud — more rocks." We mixed cement, dumped it in a wheelbarrow and shoved it to Charlie's side followed immediately by a load of rocks. Sandwiched between these jobs we started a new batch of cement. Charlie started early; no use wasting a day. And who ever heard of a coffee break?

As soon as this fireplace was completed, the one for the lounge was started. We had previously hauled boatloads of Gunflint iron formation rocks, found in quantity along the shore of Gunflint Lake, and piled them at the front door of the lodge. The Gunflint iron formation, along with other iron formations, was formed in the Precambrian period. Voyageurs used the flint they found imbedded in "our" formation for their flintlock guns.

When the children came home on weekends, Bruce heaved the rocks to Charlie. The fireplace was built in record time. As a final touch Charlie arranged selected rocks in the shape of a flintlock gun for the hearth in the lounge.

CHAPTER 6

"THE LIVES AROUND US"

Animal Orphans and Other Inhabitants

DURING my 58 years spent in this north country I had innumerable experiences with the animals who inhabit these woods. Several of the more interesting happenings are related here.

Lassoing a Moose

In the early thirties when there was easy freedom in moving back and forth across the border, Ben Ambrose was guiding Mr. Lindbloom, our guest, to Northern Light Lake, a portage to the first lake in Canada east of Saganaga Lake. Dad and I along with Doris Cole, a college classmate visiting for a couple of weeks, were invited along on the trip. We took our 16-foot wooden boat and a square-stern canoe, each with a 3-hp motor. Ben and Mr. Lindbloom were going to fish, and Doris, Dad and I were going to "explore."

We passed through island-studded Saganaga and on up the northeastern arm to the Northern Light portage. This was a short portage with a slight rise toward the center. The portage had rails with a small car on which to load a boat and push-pull the outfit to the other side. A few "railroad" portages like this one had been constructed to enable the foresters to get their equipment from one lake to another when fighting a fire.

145

After crossing the portage we motored up the narrow channel and swung into the bay where Hoof Creek terminates. We found a point which was an ideal spot for lunch. It was wooded with a few tall pines, and it had a rise, offering a good view and a comfortable breeze. Benny and Mr. Lindbloom went to the mouth of Hoof Creek to catch fish for lunch. Dad rested at the point while Doris and I poked around the bay in the boat.

A moose with its yearling calf swam out from shore to cross to the other side of the bay. I had the notion of coralling them, turning them and shepherding them back toward Dad so he could see them too. I was soon to learn that animals dislike being thwarted when they are swimming toward a specific destination.

In this instance, all I succeeded in was separating the mother and calf. The cow kept on toward the opposite shore, but I held the calf in abeyance. It refused to go toward the point where Dad was resting, as it wanted to follow its mother. I had the sudden notion that maybe we could lead it by tying a rope around its neck and gently towing it. Doris untied the painter from the boat. We made a big loop in one end, slid alongside the calf and slipped the noose over its head. Very quickly we discovered that a moose can't be steered by pulling it — it would drown first. By now the calf was heading back to its starting point. We were hanging onto the rope, and the calf was towing us in the boat.

We approached land, and I became a little apprehensive. I didn't want to leave the rope on, for fear the moose might become entangled and die. And I wasn't sure how I was going to remove it. The boat grazed the shore. The yearling calf gained its footing and started to run. I hung onto the rope trying unsuccessfully to stop the critter. I finally raced around the opposite side of a tree and halfway back again, and we came to an abrupt halt. The moose struggled to free itself. I decided the only way we could remove the rope was to "throw the calf" — I had seen it done in a rodeo. I made a lunge, threw the calf off balance, and we landed together with its rear in my lap. It was kicking furiously. I freed one of my legs, threw it over the back of the calf and tucked my foot under its haunch so it couldn't kick. There we sat stymied. If Doris let go the rope, I might be unable to hold the moose when it was released, and I'd be vulnerable to a mighty kick.

The calf started to emit resounding bawls. I thought of the trouble I would be in if Mother Moose returned to rescue her young one. Fortunately Ben and Mr. Lindbloom were returning from the mouth of the river and heard the calf. Ben saw my boat and hesitated, thinking I was imitating a calf to get him to come ashore. Fortunately for me he decided the sound was too authentic, and they landed and came to our rescue. It took both Mr. Lindbloom and Ben to disentangle the rope from the calf moose and the moose from me. As soon as the calf was released it trotted back toward the bay where it would be reunited with its mother.

Teddy the Fawn

One day while I was traveling down Gunflint Lake by boat, Charlie Anderson, who was a caretaker at a cabin halfway down the lake, hailed me into his place. Periodically he would go "dry," and he often wanted beer in a swap for labor, an unusually large fish or, in the winter, a fur.

As I pulled to shore, he said, "I'll swap you a baby fawn for a case of beer — maybe two cases."

I answered, "Charlie, where did you get a fawn?"

He replied, "I found it, something must have happened to its mother, maybe she deserted it or she was killed."

More than likely he stumbled upon the fawn, whereupon it assumed the shape of a supply of beer.

He led me to an old shed in back where a tiny spotted

Teddy with Mother

deer lay curled in a forlorn heap. Now this infant would have to be bottle fed if it were to survive. The damage was done; the barter made. We agreed he would collect his fee on his next trip up the lake. I gathered the hungry waif in my arms and carried it back to the boat. With the baby fawn riding in my lap, I steered the boat back home. We rigged a nipple on a bottle to offer it a formula of diluted canned milk, which it gulped greedily. We dubbed it Teddy.

At this time Bill and I were sleeping in the small log guest cabin. We spread papers on a portion of the floor and propped a stove baseboard against the wall. We laid a couple of old blankets in this little cove and moved Teddy in. The fawn seemed to be comfortable hiding in this dark recess. In the wild when they are strong enough to run a little, their main protection comes from taking little leaps and then lying motionless. They choose spots amid some growing or wooded covering of grass and brush so they are camouflaged.

We forgot that babies must be fed frequently, around the clock. Although we fed it when we went to bed at midnight, it was up with the breaking of dawn. It would pace back and forth clicking its tiny hoofs on the bare floor, or place a cold nose against an exposed arm. I would poke Bill, who would groan — climb out of bed and go to the lodge to start a wood fire in the range to heat a bottle of milk. When he returned we would both watch the fawn pull at the nipple with overwhelming hunger. Its large brown eyes framed with long eyelashes seemed to convey its appreciation. As its stomach swelled and it completely drained the bottle, it lost interest in food, jerked its short tail back and forth in satisfaction and quietly disappeared into its hiding place.

On one particular morning being still weary from the work of the day before, we did not respond to the clomping feet, the nudging by a wet nose and the low "ma" sound being emitted by the hungry rascal. I was roused enough to mutter, "Oh, go away and lie down," and I sleepily gave it a tap on the nose. There was a moment of silence! It suddenly made a jump and landed on top of Bill's chest with all four feet. Bill came up from a sound sleep with arms flailing. Teddy was thrown off balance, did a somersault and landed upside down between the bed and the wall, bawling and entangled in blankets. This episode awakened us completely and before peace was restored, we had to make our usual trek to the lodge to heat milk. Finally night feeding stopped.

By then, Teddy scampered around the yard all day and just slept "in" at night. One time just before dusk, a sudden storm resulted in a downpour accompanied by thunder and lightning. We feared the fawn wasn't old enough to weather this onslaught, and so clad in raingear we hunted along the trail and lakeshore calling and searching to no avail. Finally we gave up and started to return to our cabin. As we stepped off the trail, we saw it there, practically invisible, scrunched into a tiny knot and soaking wet.

Later in the spring Teddy became more independent and came to the door only to receive supplemental feedings. At the start of the season we moved from our cabin to other sleeping quarters. We gave up our cabin to guests for the summer season. The first occupants were a middle-aged couple. At six in the morning the gentleman heard a noise and called "Who's there?" There was no response so he rose and opened the door to have a spotted fawn bound into the room. The surprise was mutual.

Teddy was fond of cigarettes and pancakes, bread and milk and an assortment of food which he would take from anyone who offered it. From time to time he would gain entrance to the dining room, to the glee of the guests.

On one such occasion a guest called me and asked, "What did you say this deer's name was?"

I answered, "We call him Teddy."

With a wide grin, he said, "Your deer is misnamed."

I had never looked, but as long as *she* was around, she answered to the call of Teddy.

A Wolf

We were driving our car down the lake to put up Charlie Olson's ice, and we saw a wolf. It was crossing the lake from the Canadian side to our side. I thought if I hurried, I could intercept it. We met, and the wolf turned and ran parallel to the car, so close I could almost reach out and touch it. It ran with a sinewy grace, its tongue hanging loose. It did not run as one harassed but like a racer competing with this monster at its side. We were so interested in watching it and so intent on not hitting it, that we were unaware it was slowly crowding us toward shore. Our car hit a snowbank on shore and came to an abrupt halt. The big timber wolf with its years of survival techniques loped ahead of the car and vanished in the woods. After shoveling ourselves free of the snowbank, we returned to our task at Charlie's.

Wolves were a part of our heritage along with fox,

deer, moose, otter and beaver. They were set apart however, for they were in constant competition with man for his food. Our Indians, although they often made the threat, wouldn't shoot a wolf, let alone skin it. In their beliefs the wolf was a reincarnation of one of their ancestors.

Not so with the white man. There were the years the Dept. of Game and Fish condoned the shooting of wolves from airplanes as they sunned themselves on lakes. Wolves were trapped for bounty paid by the State of Minnesota and Canada, exclusive of sale of the hide. They became more elusive and cautious; they were seldom seen, although their tracks revealed their wanderings.

While we were having a cup of coffee at Charlie Olson's before starting the ice job, Charlie Cook told about finding a den of baby wolves whose mother had been killed. He took the babies home to raise. They were shy and hid in the bushes when strangers appeared. But alone with the family, they wrestled and played with Abie's children like any friendly puppies. After they grew up one wolf stayed with Charlie and followed him on his trapline for several winters.

Toots

In 1938 when Bruce was born there was deep snow in the woods. The deer had yarded into cedar swamps. They had almost run out of food, but they were helpless to break new trails. A local forester traveling by snowshoe was making a survey of both timber stands and deer yarding areas when he came across a young fawn that was too weak to stand. He picked it up, curled it around his shoulders and headed for our house. He laid the emaciated deer in the snow and stepped into our cabin for a cup of coffee.

We discussed the deer over steaming cups of coffee and I remarked, "I'm tied down taking care of my new baby, so

151

Toots with Bill

you might as well bring the deer in too. Perhaps I can nurse some strength into it." We spread papers on the living room floor and laid our baby deer carefully in its new habitat. Cradling its head in our arms we tried everything that we had previously fed deer. Warm milk from a bottle with nipple, oatmeal, cigarettes, sugar, pancakes, the tender new growth of cedar tips, young shoots of birch and just plain water were all offered. The fawn gazed at us with its large brown eyes and quietly laid its head back on the floor. Life, it seemed, was scarcely worth the struggle.

In a last desperate move Bill gathered wisps of bearded moss, a moss that grows in tiny clumps on live birch trees. The tiny deer took a few morsels of the frail moss between its lips.

Once I had watched a deer extend its lips and pull off some of these moss bits as if they were a necessary part of its diet. Whatever its life-giving qualities, the moss turned the tide for this deer.

For a week or 10 days Bill spent a couple of hours each morning snowshoeing from birch tree to birch tree.

At each stop he plucked an infinitesimal clump of bearded moss off a branch and dropped it into his paper sack. Had a human from the "outside" observed him snowshoeing from tree to tree plucking at bits of nothing, he surely would think it was a case of "cabin fever."

Very slowly day by day the fawn became stronger. Finally she could hold up her head and take milk. Eventually she took snitches of pancakes. One day she made a valiant effort to stand on her wobbly legs. We thereby christened her Toots.

Toots followed our every footstep with her tiny hoofs clicking across the board floor. One evening while preparing dinner, I tied Bruce's bottle of formula to the inside of his bassinet and left for the kitchen. I heard a sudden earth-shattering howl, intermixed with frustration and anger, emanating from the front room. I rushed back and found Toots' head in the bassinet lustily working on the nipple, while Bruce was objecting to the intrusion with the full force of his 6½-pound body.

Because of the deep snow Toots stayed close. She became a part of our household and spent as much time in the house as out. She relied on us for all of her nourishment. As spring approached she stayed outside day and night. The snow was almost gone, and shoots from the tulip bulbs I had planted in fall were three or four inches high.

One night I heard a nimble step outside the window, a crunch and then another crunch. My tulips! I was out of bed in a jiffy, and out the window I saw Toots in the dazzling brightness of a full moon, methodically moving down the row of tulips tastily nipping off each new shoot. I called her, and she came into the house so I went back to bed. But Toots, instead of lying down, quietly paced the floor. From the moonlit window to the back door her dainty hoofs went click, click, click across the rugless floor.

Click, click, click with a steady monotony like dripping water that becomes psychic in its repetition. After an hour of this sleepless torture I climbed out of bed and shoved the deer out. She immediately went around the house and finished clipping my row of tulips — they were born and died in the making.

The "Dead" Mink

Blanche Olliffe was a guest from the midwest who frequently visited our lodge for her summer vacation. I asked her to join me for the drive to a neighboring resort to borrow a piece of mechanical equipment. Just as we turned from our side road onto the Gunflint Trail, we noticed an inert dark object in the road. I thought it might be an injured snowshoe rabbit; they have brown fur in summer. When I passed, I realized it was a mink. I stopped to pick it up because I thought some of the guests' children might be interested in seeing it up close. A mink has soft brown fur covering its body with a splash of white under the chin.

The "Dead" Mink

It was still warm and barely breathing, but it did not seem long for this world. I laid it on the seat between us. Blanche and I drove on, and she noticed it was stirring. I carefully moved it to the back seat where it remained inert.

When we returned to the lodge the children and many adults quickly gathered around when I placed the limp mink on the counter. It was still out cold, and after inspecting it carefully I diagnosed a concussion. One guest remarked, "You might as well kill it and put it out of its misery."

"It might live — guess I'll try to help it." I answered.

I wrapped the mink in an old wool shirt and placed it in a box to await the workings of Nature. The next morning I pulled back the covering to see if my patient was still living. He opened one eye and gazed at his unfamiliar surroundings.

Blanche had become interested in the mink's survival, so she held his head while I tried in vain to give him water from an eyedropper. Two days elapsed before it would take a bit of raw hamburger from my finger and water from the eyedropper. The mink gradually became stronger and moved around more but it was obvious it had an injured hind leg. It became able to climb out of the box and get into the kitchen where it tried to stand erect to receive a handout from the cook.

Within a week the mink had regained its strength. It got around easily, aside from the small limp. I turned it loose. It became more independent each day and scurried in and out of the dry storeroom and tool shed.

A couple of weeks after the accident I met Limpy, the mink, now shy and jumpy, in the tool shed. I knelt down on the floor extending my hand toward it with a chunk of hamburger balanced on my fingertips. After making several approaches and fearful hasty retreats, it extended its neck as far as it could and quickly grabbed the chunk of meat and ran. I remained motionless. In a few minutes it came back and licked the tip of each of my fingers. With that final thank you it reverted to its wild unapproachable nature.

A Yearling Deer

It is interesting to note the relationship that sometimes prevails between a small child and a wild animal.

I was on the lake one windy day guiding guests who were fishing for lake trout. The boat rose on the swells and sank into the troughs. A short distance away we saw what looked like a stump. It was bobbing up and down in the water and yet it was so odd that we eased over there to investigate. We found a young fawn that had been separated from its mother. It swam directly for the boat when it saw us. The guests pulled in their lines, and as I came alongside, I reached down and swooped the little creature into my lap.

We took the fawn to the lodge to the dry storeroom where it could rest and dry off. We returned to the boat and finished our fishing expedition.

In the dry storeroom we kept flour, sugar, dry cereals and all such staples in large sacks. A small side room extension housed a heavy duty sewing machine we used to repair tents and packsacks. There was ample space in the room to allow movement on either side of the machine.

As I had many times before, when I nursed a deer with bottled milk, moss or pieces of pancake, I approached my newly-found waif with slow caution. I kept the sewing machine between us, as I offered food from my hand, so it would not be threatened. After a few nervous moments it became alert, stood up and made a long jump through the doorway into the large storeroom. There it would climb up on a sack and look out the window. I left food that it ate after I departed.

I kept trying to feed it by hand, for this was the only animal that had rejected my overtures. One day I was carrying Pat when I entered the storeroom. I closed the door and placed Pat on the floor inside the door. I walked to my usual place on the opposite side of the sewing machine from the curled-up deer. I held an enticing snack. The deer ignored me.

There was a stirring near the door. Pat crawled vigorously into the little room and sat down to behold the deer, inadvertently blocking the animal's escape route. The deer watched the baby and the baby watched the deer. I sat motionless, spellbound and apprehensive. Pat crawled around and sat beside the deer. It stopped chewing its cud and they peered at each other.

Pat moved closer, reached over and stuck her finger up its nostril and wiggled it vigorously. The deer remained motionless. Then she stuck her fingers in the deer's mouth in back of the front cutting teeth and wiggled its lips. They sat quietly and looked at each other.

I thought now it would surely accept food from my hand. I extended my hand ever so slowly between the bars of the machine. The deer looked at the baby, then at me. It suddenly jumped up, soared high over Pat's head, out into the other room and stood defiantly on top of a sugar sack.

I picked up the baby and walked out the door, leaving it open for the deer to return to the woods.

Charlotte Bosworth and the Bear

One fall day the lodge dining room became unexpectedly full. Since only one waitress was on duty, our longtime guest, Charlotte Bosworth jumped to her feet and proceeded to clear tables, pour water for newcomers, take orders and reset tables. In this capacity she received a 10-cent tip from two boys who had just returned from a canoe trip and had stopped for lunch. On this day she acquired the waitress nickname of "Barbara."

Dressed in high boots, knee length knickers, and a

157

small floppy plaid hat pinned up on one side with a Sierra Club pin, Charlotte hiked all the nearby trails. She carried field glasses and a bird call. She usually returned with an enumeration of the birds she had seen and occasionally the name of one to add to her "life list." She would also immediately identify various kinds of unknown plants or flowers with the aid of a reference book.

Charlotte was a voluminous writer — sending little notes to acquaintances all over the world — often thoughtfully enclosing a sheet of stamps or a "treat" to some struggling student. For Bruce, while in college, the treat in the form of a $20 bill arrived at Easter when she figured a student was usually broke.

Behind the lodge a short distance there was a live beaver pond where we set minnow traps. The beaver usually came forth in the evening or if not disturbed too frequently, they would appear in the late afternoon to check and repair their dam or seek food. Charlotte was anxious to watch a beaver at work so I suggested she accompany me on my next minnow "run." I went striding ahead, and she came behind enjoying the glimpse of a bird, listening to its song and appreciating the flowered carpet of the forest. A beaver easing quietly across the pond heard my approach, gave a resounding slap with its tail and disappeared. Although Charlotte missed the beaver, she did see a lynx with its short tail and tufted ears quietly jump onto the beaver dam and look leisurely from one side to the other. It slowly sauntered across the dam and then into the thicket beyond.

After gathering the trapped minnows we started back toward the lodge, but we stopped to listen. A couple of my sled dogs were barking persistently a short distance off the trail.

I said, "Charlotte, I think the dogs have treed a bear, shall we go and see?"

She answered, "I think that would be fun."

We turned off the trail and headed into the woods. In a short time we became enmeshed in an area of tag alder and windfalls. It was a difficult stretch to traverse and required climbing over or crawling under the felled trees and getting around their uprooted trunks. In the midst of the tangled mess Charlotte said, "I think I'll just wait here until you investigate and then you can come back and get me." With dusk descending rapidly and a bear close at hand I answered, "Sorry, but you'll have to keep moving, for it will soon be dark." We struggled on through the spreading branches and overturned roots.

Suddenly we found ourselves in the clear with the dogs barking very close by. There was no evidence of a bear in any of the surrounding trees. I pressed closer warily and discovered that the commotion was ahead of us but down on the ground. A large partially-downed cedar offered us a path of opportunity. I walked atop its sloping length and found a big black bear with beady black eyes lying directly below me and defying the two heckling dogs. The bear seemed unable to move. I led Charlotte along the tree trunk so she could see this spectacle.

It was almost dark now, and it was becoming increasingly difficult to see the faint deer trail that we were following. After we left the bear and worked our way back to the lodge along this forest trail, I kept puzzling over the fact that the bear had not run from the dogs nor gone up a tree. And I had never known dogs to run a bear down.

Back at the lodge I mentioned the unusual situation to George Plummer. He said, "I'll bet the bear got some poison out of the dump, but you never can trust a bear, though." That seemed a logical answer.

After a long discussion a number of the guests and several summer home neighbors decided on a morning safari to either help the bear in its misery or dispose of it.

The following morning we collected an assortment of materials: a rope, an axe, rifle, a bottle of strong but sweetened cathartic, cameras and a few cans for water. We headed back in the woods trailed by neighbors, guests and their children. We found the bear where we had left it, still suffering from what appeared to be a distended belly.

Bruce cut two long poles. He and Paul Schoenoff, a neighbor, each took a pole and formed a straight triangle that pinned down the bear's head. I made a small lasso at the end of a rope, crawled forward and slipped it over a hind leg. I did the same with the other hind leg and tied the rope ends to nearby trees. I worked forward and followed the same procedure for the front legs. We then had the helpless bear spread-eagled before us, and we felt safe from any quick and dangerous move that it might make. Someone brought forth the quart bottle of cathartic. Paul placed it between the bear's lips and let the contents gurgle down its throat. Charlotte, who wore a pair of dainty short white gloves embroidered with colorful rosettes, leaned over and massaged the sparsely-haired swollen belly. We stood looking at our handiwork wondering what to do next. Since the bear had seemingly enjoyed the liquid diet that Paul had offered, he refilled the jug with water from a nearby depression, for we were in a moist cedar swamp. He poured this down the bear's mouth. The bear seemed to have a great craving for liquid.

Then Mat, who was taking pictures, ran out of flashbulbs and started back to the lodge for more. I called after her, "There is a little bit of whiskey in a bottle under the counter; bring that too." While we waited for her return, we decided the bear was too weak to move. It would be more comfortable if it could at least roll over and be right side up. Warning the children to stay back because of the unpredictableness of a bear, we released the ropes one by one. The bear rolled over and watched the surrounding onlookers. One of the neighbors filled a can from a nearby spring. I offered this to the bear, and it drank greedily, in the manner of a thirsty hard-driven horse.

Mat returned with the Scotch. I placed the bottle between the bear's lips and poured the contents into its mouth. Perhaps the liquid was bitter or the bear a teetotaler, but quick as a flash it lunged and grabbed the nearest object, which happened to be my leg, between its teeth. Almost at the same instant I sprang backward, lost my balance and fell flat on my back. The surrounding crowd was momentarily frozen in its tracks. We had left the gun leaning against a tree on the far side of the bear.

Fortunately the bear didn't have the strength to pursue the attack, nor the strength in its jaws to tear out a chunk of flesh. It left, instead, two deep tooth gashes, which took a couple of weeks to drain and heal and made a tetanus shot necessary. The ribbing I received from the natives was more devastating than the wound.

The crowd watching the bear was suddenly sobered from their light-hearted excursion and withdrew quickly. Later in the day Bruce returned to the site with a couple of new guests. They watched from a respectful distance while the bear groaned and rolled with the agony incurred by its distended belly and medicinal treatment.

We felt a sick bear so close to the lodge was too dangerous. We planned to go out the following morning and kill it. Perhaps the quart of physic exploded with the force of a jet and sent the bear sailing through the woods, for it was nowhere to be found. And it never reappeared.

Memorable Guests

We became so close to the guests who came year after year that we felt we were one large family. These early guests were a special breed. They accepted with aplomb the rocky gravel road — with its zigs and zags, ups and downs — as well as the gas lanterns, outside biffys and woodburning stoves.

In 1939 we started a winter business featuring dog team rides and snowshoe treks with winter cookups. Even a downhill ski run through the woods — we cleared the original Gunflint Trail right-of-way that went from the top of Gunflint Hill, across our side road and down to the lake. After coming down the hill the guests skied to a nearby boat landing. There we picked them up with tow ropes behind the car and pulled them to the top of the hill for another run. The facilities were a far cry from present sophisticated ski resorts, but there was a togetherness among all the guests and ourselves.

In winter the Gunflint Trail was precarious. There was always a possibility of getting stuck en route or of getting

Winter Guests and Winter Sports

snowed in before the county plows came our way. As I bought groceries at Ed Toftey's store in Grand Marais for our winter guests, he shook his head in disbelief. How could I, an "outsider," get people to come to the back country in the middle of winter on the pretext of having fun. These times were before the popularity of crosscountry skiing and groomed trails, of inside plumbing and cabins maintained at constant temperatures, or head bolt heaters for cars and roads plowed to the door. But they were special times for special people.

The majority of winter guests who first came to the lodge were from Duluth and Minneapolis-St. Paul. There were times when a party came by bus to Grand Marais and we met them with our car.

One winter day I started for town to pick up a couple. The road had not been plowed recently, but there was a good track to follow until I reached The Pines. The three miles from this point to Grandma Hedstrom's Corner was devoid of trees as a fire had burned this section clean a few years before. It was like a prairie where the wind swept unhindered filling all depressions with snow. The snow-filled track was barely discernible. I started shoveling to clear a path. It became routine: shovel 25 feet and move up the car; do another 25 feet and move it again.

I was soon joined by Alex Dominisky, a neighbor, who was heading back to his army camp. He had to get out for he was to be shipped overseas in another few days. Shoveling was easier now. We each shoveled one rut and moved the cars up at a faster pace. The wind had let up, so I was gambling I could drive back on my own tracks later that day.

When we were almost a mile from the magic corner, I had had enough shoveling to last me a lifetime. Alex and I stood discussing the pros and cons of getting through, when a big truck appeared coming up from town. It was Don Brazell.

When Bill had not received a call from me, he called Don and asked him to drive up and look for me. Don pulled up and stuck his head out the cab window. He said to me, "By God, I never thought I would see you stuck and giving up." Alex and I got in our cars and gleefully followed Don's track back to town.

Alex went on to the war from which he would never return. I met my party in town and did an about face. The road was as good as I hoped; the single track had not filled in. After we reached The Pines, it was clear sailing. I stopped at Carl Brandt's on Poplar Lake to call Bill and tell him to put the coffee pot on; I'd be home within the hour.

It was not to be, for going around a curve I slithered hopelessly off the road. There was no option but to hike back to Carl's where we slept that night on the floor. It took most of the next day and all our ingenuity to get the car back on the road. Fortunately the couple thought it an exciting experience.

These guests and many others came to enjoy the north-woods in winter — despite the inconveniences and simple accommodations. We took them on day trips with a cozy fire and a noon cookup. We were with our guests on most of the trips, which insured their being comfortable in the woods. In the evening there were song fests or outdoor treasure hunts. In our remote location, the cares of the world seemed to evaporate.

The Jaques

One Wilderness Express trip at the end of October brought Florence and Lee Jaques to stay until late January. Florence was to write a book on her experience living in the northwoods while Lee spent his days working on illustrations for a new book to be published the following year. He worked both with a scratch board and with water-colors. His works in watercolors had the appearance of oils.

At first I was self-conscious wondering what Florence was writing about, and what were her reactions to us. But after a couple of days I figured, the heck with it; for better or worse they would have to accept us as we were. The Jaques arrived during deer hunting season. We kept the lodge open for hunting and used it again for guests over the Christmas holidays. The lodge had been built for summer use, with little insulation. It took a large supply of wood to keep the stoves stoked full. Lee tried a few days of hunting. He shot his first and last deer as he found it was not a sport he enjoyed.

The Jaques slept and worked in one of our guest cabins. After the hunters left and we closed the lodge, they came to our home to join our family for meals. They graciously accepted the odors that seemed to sift through the cabin when I was cooking dog food. Only when I inadvertently opened the fox scent Bill had for trapping, did they draw the line. When I pulled the cork the bottle exploded, and the contents hit the ceiling. I spent hours scrubbing with ammonia water to reduce the odoriferous taint in the air.

In our country way we set out to celebrate New Year's with our neighbors. Although the temperature was way below zero, life took on a rosy glow after some hot rum toddies. We built a fire under the oil pan of the car, and it sputtered and started. We shoveled a roadway alongside the dock where snow had drifted, so we could drive out on the frozen lake. By the time we accomplished all this it was close to midnight on New Year's Eve. We piled in the car with loaded rifles and buzzed across the ice-covered lake

Florence Jaques with Bill at the Trapping Shack

waking our neighbors, Val and Ben Ambrose, to a Happy New Year accentuated with rifle shots.

A few days later Sue and Andy Mayo, from Sea Gull, came wheeling in their new contraption to give the Jaques and us a ride. Since they lived down Sea Gull Lake about six miles with no road, Andy rigged up an old Ford so they could travel across the lake even when the ice was covered with snow.

It was a precursor to the snowmobile. He replaced the front wheels with a pair of skis and added an idler wheel ahead of the chain-covered rear wheels. The vehicle would travel up to 30 miles an hour. Although they seldom drove it that fast, it carried a load of groceries and was faster than snowshoeing pulling a toboggan.

Many evenings during the Jaques' stay were spent in various games and activities. One game we played often was Anagrams. Their extensive and seemingly inexhaustible vocabulary often led to our defeat.

One evening Florence and I painted our own master-pieces in watercolors with Lee as the judge of the winner. We took great pains on our works and submitted them to our "judge." A quizzical smile passed over his face as he remarked, "I think you had better stay with writing."

Perhaps one of the greatest tributes which can be given to the Jaques, who had no children of their own, is that after living and eating in close proximity with our family of two people and their small youngsters for several months, we were all mutually sorry to part. They were an exceptional couple. Their book about that winter experience, *Snowshoe Country,* is now in its sixth printing.

Snowshoe Country, Florence Page Jaques, illustrations by Francis Lee Jaques, The University of Minnesota Press, Minneapolis, Minn., 1944.

CHAPTER 7

"LIVING TOGETHER IN THE FOREST"

S PARSELY located as we were, there developed within us an unspoken, hidden concern for a neighbor's safety. This feeling, call it what you may, permeated the fiber of the people who lived in this remote area for a long time. We gave help with no thought of being repaid by trinkets — whether beads, shells, coins or some other means of exchange. Help was given as a mutual means of survival in a demanding and often uncompromising environment. It was an exchange where deep within one's soul resided an element of trust one to the other.

In this spirit the following incidents occurred.

Butchie to the Rescue

By the late 1950s, snowmobiles had replaced dog teams for winter transportation along the Gunflint Trail. I had a little 3-hp Polaris and I often took rides to escape household chores and to relax — much like city folks would take a Sunday afternoon drive in a car.

This day was sunny, windless but cold. I stopped across the lake to ask Butchie to accompany me to the end of Gunflint Lake and maybe as far as North Lake. She had a cold and felt more comfortable staying in her warm log cabin.

I drove at a leisurely pace to the end of the lake and

followed a well-used snowmobile trail over the old railroad spur that once carried white pine logs to Thunder Bay. Three quarters of the way up Little Gunflint Lake, the trail swung across to the American side to avoid a rapids that remained open all winter. Little North Lake had a frozen narrows where snowmobiles had been traveling, but which carried a current that made the crust unpredictable and deceptive. The ice suddenly gave way, submerging my machine but leaving it balanced on a ledge that dropped into deeper water.

This early Polaris Playmate had two parts joined with one long rod. Since I was unable to pull the whole thing out, I pulled the rod that made the machine one entity. Then I pulled out the rear unit with motor and tracks, and finally, the front with the attached skis. On shore I joined the two parts, gave the starter rope a pull, and the engine caught and purred. Wet beyond my waist and with my woolen clothes fast forming a frozen crust, I hopped on my trusty "steed" and retraced my route.

Early Snowmobile, Polaris Playmate, 1958

After about a mile the water which had seeped into the gas tank made its presence known. The motor died halfway across Little Gunflint.

Was it ESP or that compatible feeling between individuals that draws one to the rescue of another person for no particular reason?

Butchie felt uneasy after about an hour (which was about the time I went through the ice), and she thought I might be in trouble. She dressed especially warm to thwart her cold, started her Bombadier snowmobile and followed my tracks.

She found me trudging toward the railroad bed after abandoning my snowmobile back on the ice. Her greeting was simple. "I thought you might have trouble, I come."

She also had dry matches and the know-how to kick the snow aside, gather wood and start a fire in the time it took me to shed my frozen clothes. The fire burned lustily as I stood on a pad of balsam boughs and revolved slowly as if I were baking on a spit. Butchie dried my clothes — almost. Instead of being wet they had a warm dampness. I rode behind Butchie on her machine and she whisked me the eight miles back up Gunflint Lake as the accelerated north wind whipped up spirals of snow that stung our faces with relentless persistence.

Waste Nothing

Another day I took a trip to Saganaga with the Polaris. This frozen lake was covered with snowy trails. The main trail went directly up the inside passage to the Canadian side of the lake, and then branched off to Dorothy Powell's resort named Chippewa Inn. Another spur led to Dinna and Art Madsen's resort, Camp Sagonto, and a spider web of trails led to cabins where a handful of people spent vacations both winter and summer.

I followed one branch to visit Irv and Tempest Benson who operated their Pine Island camp in the summer and trapped in the winter. During our conversation Irv recounted the following story demonstrating the unwritten rule that each person takes only what he needs from nature's bounties and wasted nothing:

"On October 16th, Tempest had spent a rather full morning and part of the afternoon washing clothes while I was operating a long-handled shovel down at the garden and in my beloved compost pile. Along about 2 pm Tempest came down and mentioned it might be a good idea to make a run down to Curran Bay to see if we could ambush a deer. Nothing could have sounded better at the moment.

In an hour's time we had tied up the boat at the Northern Light rapids turnoff and started paddling down into the bay in a 13-foot canoe we had towed along. The wind was at our backs. The idea was to sit down there in the lower part of the bay and watch for anything that might come out. Just as we entered the wide part of the bay both of us noticed a dim black object amongst the shore brush, and before we could stop the canoe, a young bull moose walked slowly down to the shore and started swimming across the bay some 200 yards ahead and 100 yards to our left.

Almost immediately 'bull hungry,' [referring to Tempest] in the stern of the canoe, made a wonderful and most successful attempt to make the canoe plane. About the same time the moose decided that the air where he had been was preferable to that where he was heading, and he turned back to the shore he had just left. Tempest's washing activities had evidently done more for her than my compost burrowing had done for me, and moose have delicate nostrils.

We had quite a discussion before the animal reached shore. Tempest was all for substituting moose steak for our anticipated deer meat, but I had visions of our freezer at home chockful of chicken and weiners. Orders from the stern of the canoe consistently maintained shoot-shoot-shoot as the bull climbed on shore. I held off until

171

we noticed, that regards to being fat he was just about as round as he was long. Had the animal been a cow instead of a bull, I wouldn't have been surprised to see it wear a girdle.

There was time for two fast shots and either both hit or the moose tripped over the big 338 nozzler slugs and died when he fell hitting his head on a rock. Within a half hour the cleaning operation was completed and we were on our way back to the tied-up boat. The carcass was left in the hide unskinned for the night to enable the meat to cool slowly. The following day we returned to butcher the animal. The moose remnants unsuitable for freezing were canned, and all bones were roasted to save the remaining meat on them for soup and soup stock. Dogs ate the innards and the innards' innards went into the compost pile. The only thing left in Curran Bay was a hole in the air where the moose had been."

I rode on down to Frank and Betsy Powell's resort and was invited in for tea and cookies. Frank once had a "Jenny," of WWI vintage. The entire frame of the plane was wood including the spars and struts of the wings. The

Frank Powell's "Standard," Summer 1930

authorities grounded the plane when all wooden frame aircraft were condemned in the early 1930s in Canada.

Frank was a good pilot and flew all over the lakes with it, patching a rip as needed with a beaver hide needle and thread or a piece of tape.

One cold, crisp, starlit night following a heavy snow, I went buzzing along the Gunflint Trail to pick up Peggy Heston, a neighbor. The side roads had become plugged by snow, so we gave up our cars and reverted to snowmobiles until our turn came for the hard-pressed plow and crew. Peggy was on her way back from town where she had been with her husband, Myrl, who was in the hospital recovering from a heart attack. She had caught a ride to Tuscarora Lodge and needed a ride home to Heston's Lodge on Gunflint Lake. I cranked up my Playmate, hooked on my ancient dog team sled and scooted to Tuscarora.

Since Peggy had been in town, she wore a pair of slacks and a fancy sweater; I doubt if there was long underwear underneath. The Tuscarora owners rigged her out in an oversize parka with a fur-lined hood, trousers, mitts and overshoes.

We made a ludicrous sight — these two women on a pony-size snowmobile streaking along the Trail on a nippy night. One was clad in a heavy Cowichan sweater with red tassle cap flying, the other buried in a fur-fringed parka hood with only a tiny pink nose protruding. Gliding along behind came the sled loaded with sacks of corn for the deer who came in daily for a handout.

CHAPTER 8

"CHANGING TIMES"

Environment and Wildlife

THIS land was once covered with towering white pine and heavy stands of norway pine. Under this shaded canopy there was little underbrush making cross country travel easy. Logging camps were established and the big pines logged off.

A Canadian railroad was built from Port Arthur (now part of Thunder Bay) past such settlements as Silver Mountain, Addie Lake, North Lake, Le Blaine, Gunflint, and across the Cow-O-Bob-E-Cock Narrows to the Paulson mine on the Minnesota side of the international border. As the railroad was extended to the Paulson mine, bunkhouses and messhalls were rafted up Gunflint Lake and anchored

Towing the Messhall, 1921

174

next to the shore on the west side of the narrows to accommodate the men building the railroad.

Investors from New York came up the wagon road by buckboard from Grand Marais to the Paulson mine. (A short distance from the Gunflint Trail side road, parts of this old trail can still be found.)

Fires followed the logging operations — the trestles and bridges along the railroad burned and were never replaced. No one paid attention to the fires in the wilderness country.

The loss of the big pines was followed by growth of birch, aspen, jack pine, spruce and balsam. The tall canopy was gone, and thick stands of tag alder and moose maple worked their way in between the trees. Then the country became known as the bush country — the term is still used.

There were people who came and replaced the Indians. There was a gradual build up of cabins on a sprinkling of lakes where private property was available for purchase or lease from the State of Minnesota or the U.S. government. These new residents were mostly conservationists who wanted to enjoy the woods and all it had to offer including the wildlife that chanced to be about.

In 1958 the Long Year Mining Co. brought in some big drilling equipment and did considerable testing in the area of Tucker Lake, Loon Lake, Mayhew Lake, Magnetic Bay and Magnetic Rock Trail. Some of the exploratory drilling went as deep as 1200 feet, and every snitch of the core was recovered. The only comment I ever heard about the outcome of the drilling was from a University of Minnesota geologist who once asked me, "How would you like to have a smelter within five miles of your place?" I shuddered at the thought.

Over these years the amount of wildlife flowed and ebbed. The caribou had vanished. Deer became more abundant than moose. Porcupine and skunk were everywhere. As the porcupines' favorite food, the inner bark of coniferous trees, diminished they became more scarce and finally disappeared perhaps due to their enemy, the fisher. The pine marten became scarce when the demand for its fur increased. They are easily trapped and can be quickly eliminated. The snowshoe rabbit and fox seem to cycle together. Beaver have been heavily trapped and in some places fight for survival. The number of wolves vary with the deer population. The loons appear to be holding their own, returning each year.

For the wildlife, there is an ever changing ecological surge or scarcity depending on rain, high or low waters, amount of snow and severity of winters.

Travel

The usual modes of traveling in winter were to use snowshoes or a dog team if you had one. Dog teams were trained to follow the driver and the snowshoe trails. They were used on traplines and would stop at each set like a horse on a milk route.

Winter travel was slow, so when Walter Plummer went to his trapping grounds at Mowe Lake, he would stay from the end of October until Christmas. After Walter's death, when George Plummer trapped those same grounds, he'd snowshoe over — a seven and a half hour trip — stay a few days and then snowshoe back. On one of these return trips, he was given a ride by Ernie Sitch, a Saganaga Lake resident who drove a homemade snowmobile. George became entranced with the ease of travel by snowmobile — as we all did. Snowmobiles became common on the Trail by 1958.

My undoing came when salesmen interested Art Schliep of Clearwater Lodge in trying a Polaris Playmate. This little machine had about a 3-hp motor in the rear. The skis were held onto the body with one long bolt. The seat was a covered board which could hold two riders. I jumped at Art's offer to try it. I went down the lake to the Mountain Lake portage, walked across the portage and returned, all within the hour. It was a new and exciting experience.

I purchased a little Polaris like Art's. Charlie Cook and Butchie each purchased a Canadian Bombadier, with a 5-hp motor.

From that time on Butchie and Charlie and I followed the dog team trails. We chugged along not much faster than the dogs had traveled, but we kept a steady pace with no dog fights.

The surrounding trees absorbed the sound. Only when we held our ears close to the ground could we "feel" the pulse and know a member of our group was still coming.

Some days we would go part way on the trapping trail, then take our snowshoes to look at one of their beaver traps at a nearby pond, stop at a sunny spot, build a fire and cook a pot of tea.

In this country it is necessary to have an established trail to operate a snowmobile, for one can't go over windfalls, rock piles or deep snow without becoming bogged down. We traveled many miles at a pace so slow we never failed to notice and identify the animal tracks that paralleled or crossed the trail or an odd formation on a twisted tree.

Suddenly there was an explosion and everyone had a snowmobile. Families took their children for winter picnics. Couples spent part of a weekend fishing on a nearby or sometimes a remote lake. The woods and lakes had become, not only a summer playground, but a winter recreation area as well.

The first machines were small, had limited horsepower and could easily follow a dog team trail. The small machines were replaced with bigger machines. Each year snowmobiles became faster and more powerful. The big snowmobiles operated most successfully down the lakes and over the portages. They were too large for the crooked dog team trails; they were built to go 60 miles an hour.

The large snowmobiles could whiz from Moose Lake, in the Ely area, to Saganaga in a day or from Squires Landing, Canada (near Thunder Bay) to Gunflint and back in a day. There were few lakes that weren't crisscrossed by snowmobile tracks. The contrast between these larger machines and the ones we drove was like comparing a race-car to a "tin Lizzy" Ford.

Snowmobiling on lakes wasn't always just a joyous run. There were slush pockets, where a machine could bog down and, unless fast action was taken, freeze in on the spot. If help were needed, the machine would have to be left suspended on timber brought from the shore while the rider hiked back by snowshoe. (We never had that experience when driving a dog team.)

One day when Butchie and I went over the winter portage to Granite Lake, we crossed Magnetic Bay en route. We whizzed by a slush spot which had an ominous look. On our return I questioned a return trip on the same route, but Butchie thought it might be safe. She led the way back and crossed the brink with safety. But as I followed, the crust gave way. I looked to one side into a yawning abyss. A large surface hole, four feet in diameter, had opened alongside the trail. It was bordered by a two- to three-inch layer of slush ice, below which were 24 inches of water.

The machine was like a dog trying to get out of a bad hole. The skis were on the trail while the rest of the machine hung in water three feet from the "eye" that beckoned a watery grave. Butchie rushed back to help. We decided that Butchie could stand on the trail and press the throttle gently. I could stand on the ledge in kneedeep water and, if the ice would hold me long enough, heave the rear of the machine forward. It worked. Except that Butchie, in her excitement, pressed the throttle too hard. I received a complete shower. And the machine took off in a circle into more slush ice with Butchie doggedly hanging on.

A couple of days later we returned. Fresh snow had fallen, and although the booby trap was still there, it was completely hidden.

CHAPTER 9

"REFLECTIONS"

The Environmental Years, 1960-1985

THE years of 1960 to 1985 were filled with trauma, uncertainties and turmoil. In the early 60s a new wilderness bill was introduced by Senator Hubert Humphrey. When this bill was finally passed in 1964, it forced all summer homeowners and commercial establishments within the BWCA to sell their properties to the government. The U.S. Forest Service was assigned to carry this out. Buildings were sold to private individuals for removal or were destroyed. This bill also gave the Forest Service a future power to curtail the use of motors on some lakes where they had customarily operated.

Those of us who were operating resorts then were assured that the restrictions imposed at this time would be final. We all had family-oriented resorts located on the perimeter of the BWCA and we made the adaptations necessary to abide by the new regulations. Many of the displaced people sought property along the lakeshore outside of BWCA boundaries.

In a short time the Forest Service outlawed motors on lakes adjacent to the international boundary waters. This affected a few resorts along the Trail whose clientele traveled over a couple of portages to a larger lake and used a canoe and motor for a day of fishing and relaxation. It also affected canoeists using three-horse motors on the big

180

waters along the border route. They were not allowed to possess a motor while making a return circle through adjacent BWCA lakes even though the motor went unused.

And it became impossible to take a motor across a larger lake, such as Saganaga, cache it on a tiny island while canoeing smaller lakes, and retrieve it on one's return. The moral fiber of the entire country had changed, and the repercussions finally reached this "no-longer-isolated back country." What had once been a sacred trust was now ignored — a cache left in the woods was invariably stolen if it were discovered.

On the Gunflint Trail, a number of people had purchased property and built summer homes on the mainland and islands in Sea Gull and Saganaga Lakes. Within the confines of this area, on Sea Gull Lake were also two small family-oriented resorts. All of these places were eliminated under the right of eminent domain. In many instances a cabin site became a campground for canoeists. Tents replaced buildings as one group of people displaced another.

The ideal proposed by the act was to travel through the country without leaving a trace. But it is impossible to use these interlocking waterways without leaving an imprint. Wherever man travels — by foot over the age-old portages or unsuccessfully running a rapids by canoe — he leaves his mark: artifacts found among the waterwashed rocks; forest fires sweeping the country from campfires carelessly left unattended.

In 1977 new regulations were proposed to have the BWCA become a wilderness area entailing new restrictions and regulations. There followed in 1978 a controversial campaign which entailed hearings in Washington. As a member of Concerned Citizens of Cook County, I made several trips to Washington to testify before Congressional committees and to contact congressmen. We were fighting for our right to exist and for the rights of other visitors, who were not canoeists, to appreciate and enjoy, in day trips, this north woods country. The Sierra Club and other organizations were fighting for a wilderness area for canoeists and campers only. The battle became a glorified political football.

The political inequities, dependent on some participants' clout or contacts, resulted in some odd regulations. On a small lake along the Gunflint Trail where a three-horse motor would be adequate, a 25-horse is allowed. On many large lakes riparian to the BWCA, motor horsepower is restricted or motors are banned.

To me the greatest travesty of all is the ruling that if one resort on a lake riparian to the BWCA elects to sell to the government, then all private homeowners on that lake must offer their property to the government first before selling to a private individual. I believe it is a violation of the rights of the other property owners for the actions of one property owner on a lake to determine the futures of all the others.

The ultimate result was the changing of the BWCA to a wilderness classification and the reinterpretation of many long-established treaties.

In my opinion, one of the most unfortunate results of this battle is the deep mistrust which has developed between resort operators and so-called conservationists. Some friendships of longstanding were torn asunder.

Since as a resort operator, I was one of those pointed at as a "despoiler," I could not help but reminisce:

In the 1930s when lake trout fish fry were available for plantings, the aerated trucks from the French River hatchery near Duluth came only as far as Grand Marais. I met this truck with my own small pickup truck. I loaded my truck with milk cans of fish fry and drove the 50 miles of hilly rocky road back to Gunflint stopping to aerate the water at every known spring along the route. I arrived with minimal loss and planted the fish in Gunflint Lake. These plantings benefitted not only me, but, also served to stock many connected lakes. Later on the hatchery trucks came halfway up the Trail which made the trip easier.

Much later I helped plant walleyes in several outlying lakes. It is true I did this to increase the fishing capacity of Gunflint Lake, but it in turn was feeding innumerable interconnecting lakes in the BWCA, as the water of one lake funnels into another. There came a time when the walleyes, a species introduced to these waters, made their spawning run on Cross River leading into Gunflint Lake. Fishermen, waiting to make a killing, would line the banks. Finally I prevailed upon the operator of the French River hatchery, who was influential at that time, to curtail fishing on the river during spawning. This natural spawning area has since been off limits to fishermen during the "hatch."

Years ago most ducks on the lakes were mergansers, known as fish ducks. Don Lobdell, who operated Rockwood Lodge on Poplar Lake, had connections with the McGraw Game Farm in Dundee, Illinois and undertook transporting mallards to the Gunflint Trail. The Minnesota Game and Fish Dept. arranged to ship mallard ducklings to Don. Some of us along the Trail agreed to raise and release the ducklings, and we built houses with fenced enclosures. Several hundred baby ducks were shipped to Duluth and Don met them with his car. He transported them to Rockwood Lodge which became the distribution center. We took 75 of these little balls of fluff and coddled, fed and pampered them. When they were a few weeks old they were banded by Charlie Ott, one of the game wardens. It was a program repeated for three years. The banded ducks who survived the firing line on their southward flight, returned each year to raise a new brood in the area.

Now mallards return each year. They build their nests under cabins and proudly display their young ones. Like bear who learn the location of a campsite and move in for a feast, so the ducks with their broods panhandle along shore, stopping at the resorts and summer homes where they are fed. Some of the birds winter in Grand Marais where they bob around in the icy waters of Lake Superior.

Hunting and trapping seasons — beaver, deer, partridge, moose, fisher and mink — have been determined by the DNR headquarters. When a particular species has become scarce in an area where hunting and trapping is encouraged I have fought, not always successfully, to have a closed season in the affected location. In some areas, the delicate balance of game, natural predators, and available food is difficult to maintain when the pressure of hunting is added. I have been told many times that wolves only take the weak and ailing. If that is true, then the "sick" moose and deer that I have seen pursued by wolves were going pell-mell. It would appear to me more likely that they had been "cut out" and isolated from their group, thus becoming more vulnerable.

Occasionally inexperienced people wander from their campsites and become lost. By the time a member of their party reaches a resort seeking help, an organized night search is required. Resort guides, boats, motors and staff members turn out to help with the search.

In the late 70s the Gunflint Trail Rescue Squad was organized. It consists of an ambulance and well trained volunteers — resort owners and homeowners on the Trail. Members of this group transport not only ailing resort guests but also seriously injured campers from the road head to the hospital in Grand Marais. In winter, rescuers use snowmobiles and snowshoes with a specially-designed rescue toboggan to transport injured persons to the road and ambulance where more sophisticated assistance is available.

Innumerable times some of us on the Trail, whether men or women, have manned fire pumps or hauled pails of water to extinguish a fire left by a careless camper. During a particularly dangerous "fire season," privately owned boats and motors were made available to the Forest Service. Housing and meals have often been supplied to fire fighters and pilots operating "water bombers."

Each spring along the Gunflint Trail, homeowners and resorters gather and walk in small groups, a pre-arranged section of the 50 miles, to pick up cans and refuse from the sides of the road. "Clean-up" participants include residents of all ages from teenagers to many people in their 60s and 70s. While I have been picking up cans from ditches, I have had a carload of people pitch a pop can out of the car window for me to pick up.

I, along with the residents on the Trail, have pressured the Forest Service to keep their clear cut logging activities screened from the Trail with a narrow no-cut buffer zone. Many of the logged-over areas are being replanted by the Forest Service in preparation for a future crop. As a result of their cooperation, the Trail remains a thing of beauty without denying loggers their harvest.

The BWCAW has now acquired a wilderness status and more restrictive measures. There were resorts who again adapted to the new regulations. They instigated naturalist programs and hired staff to develop them. For winter use cross country ski trails were developed apart from the snow-mobile trails approved by the Forest Service. Several resorts "threw in the sponge" figuring the increasing restrictions weren't worth the worry of an uncertain future.

All of the controversy over the wilderness act resulted in a huge publicity campaign. Canoeists poured in as if a new gold mine had been discovered and they each wanted a nugget. After the first surge, the subsequent years with increased restrictions have shown a steady decline in the number of canoeists using the available water routes.

The question arises. Can the boundary waters still be a stimulating experience for vacationers who through fear, handicap or age do not enjoy canoeing or camping? How will we ultimately be allowed to appreciate this great expanse of Boundary Waters?

The pendulum swings ever further — where it will stop no one knows.

GLOSSARY

A-shaped tents — One of the first canoe trip tents used. Erected with two sets of crossed poles, front and back, each pair tied together at their apex. A ridgepole was placed between the two uprights creating an elongated A frame to which the tent was attached.

airtight stove — An upright oval-shaped stove constructed of a light tin-like metal. It has a single opening on the top for putting in wood and a single regulatory draft near the bottom. The top is flat to serve as a cooking area. These stoves were used extensively by trappers because they were lightweight and they heated up quickly.

ash hoop — Oval framework made from ash poles and used for drying beaver hides. Two five-foot small-diameter ash poles were bent into U shapes and fastened together with meter line at the overlap. The hide was stretched and sewn inside this frame.

backdraft — Airflow created by a forest fire being driven forward by a wind, which causes the fire to move backward at the same time.

backwater — Eddy on the edges of a fast-flowing rapids which spin off in a U shape opposite the direction of the rapids' current.

balsam boughs — Smaller branches removed from the main branches of a balsam tree. In cold weather, these could be broken off and were used to sit or lie on.

balsam bough bed — A deluxe bed was constructed from the tips of balsam boughs, stood upright in a tight formation, making a springy mat. Most beds, however, were made from piles of boughs.

bannock — Trappers' substitute for loaf bread. A flat patty fried in a pan.

bearded moss — (class *Mucis*) Light grey moss growing in small loose clusters on live birch trees.

beaver blanket — Extra large beaver hide, when stretched and dried, called 'blanket' on the fur market.

beaver dam — A dam constructed by beaver from sticks and mud to plug a creek, creating a pond suitable for their habitation.

beaver house — Slightly cone-shaped home built by beaver out of poplar sticks and mud. Often built along the shore, but are also found in the center of a shallow pond.

beaver trap — A metal trap with jaws about eight inches across, usually having teeth. Some traps have a double spring and no teeth.

biffy — Outhouse, an outside toilet. A building with toilet seats located over an open pit.

Bi-jou — An Indian greeting word meaning "hello."

birch bark — Outer bark of a birch tree (*Petula popyrifora*) which is shed at certain times of the year. It is very inflammable and is good kindling. Sheets of a deeper layer can be peeled off in June, without killing the tree, to make birchbark baskets, tepees or canoes.

birchbark basket — Basket made of birch bark, folded and sewn with split spruce root. The basket is waterproof and lasts for years.

blackflies — (*Simuliidae*) Biting gnats that make no noise, hang in a swarm around the head, especially in thick woods. They like to bite in dark areas under tight clothing, collars, cuffs, etc. The bites cannot be felt but result in itchy welts.

border lakes — The interconnecting waterway which became the international border between Ontario and the U.S.

border patrol — Customs and Immigration officers making occasional trips from the formal border crossing at Pigeon River along the border waterway.

Boundary Waters Canoe Area Wilderness (BWCAW) — One million, thirty-one thousand plus acres of northeastern Minnesota woods and lakes restricted by federal law to remain in their primitive state.

bow paddler — Person sitting in the front of the canoe and paddling.

bull cook — In logging camps, the man who hauled in wood and water for cooking and kept the table set.

bull it — To do a task by muscular force.

bunk — Bed used in most trapping cabins. The frame is made of logs with smaller poles placed crossways and balsam boughs piled on top.

burl — Large excrescence swelling like a wart on the side of a tree trunk.

bush country — Area which has been logged, and the young growth has grown up as thick brush.

Bush Line — Improvised telephone line connecting the resorts who did not have telephones to those who did have phone service. Calls could be relayed onto the Bush Line.

CCC Camps — Civilian Conservation Corps — Program sponsored during the depression by the federal government to give forestry work to young men from cities.

cabin fever — (bunk bound) Condition of lethargy and eccentricity, seen in one who is confined to a cabin for a long time, being unable to get out and commute with other people because of inclement weather.

cache — Deposit of hidden traps or food in the woods, to be used later.

Calvert School — School in Baltimore MD, est. 1897, offering sophisticated home study courses, used primarily by parents in overseas service or in remote areas.

Canadian-Minnesota border — The international border separating Canada and the United States. See *border lakes*.

canoe — Long thin watercraft, originally made by Indians from birch bark covering cedar ribs, which craft were very frail and tippy. The birchbark covering was later replaced by canvas; the cedar frame retained. These have been replaced by craft made entirely of aluminum.

canoe outfitters — Business catering to canoeists by supplying canoes, camping equipment, dehydrated food, maps, routes and instruction.

canoe ribs — Strips of cedar, steamed and bent to create a framework for a birchbark (and later canvas-covered) canoe. The cambrian layer of the cedar tree was stripped into 2½-inch by ½-inch thick pieces.

caribou moss — (family *Musci*) One of the main foods for the woodland caribou, who used to roam this region until about 1920.

cased hides — Hides are cut between the hind legs. The legs are skinned out and then the entire hide is pulled off wrong side to like pulling off a turtleneck sweater. The hide is dried on a hide stretcher.

cedar slab — Hewed thick slice of cedar, taken from outside the main core and used for making paddles.

cedar swamp — Moist ground where cedar grows profusely and almost exclusively, and moose and deer like to feed.

chaff — Loosened husks from parched rice, when separated from the grain.

chain saw — Portable saw with a gasoline engine, used for cutting wood and which replaced crosscut saws in the late 1940s.

Chippewa — synonymous with Ojibwa — Of the Algonquian tribes as determined by linguistic similarities. Language spoken by our Indian neighbors.

chuck — Food taken on a camping trip.

clear cut — Logging with large equipment and cutting all growth, leaving the land bare except for severed stumps.

clearing house — House where furs were collected prior to sending them to the fur sales in Winnipeg and New York.

cook stove — Wood-burning stove especially for cooking, which has a cast iron top that holds heat for a long time.

Cowichan sweater — Sweater made by the Indians of British Columbia. It is made from natural wool yarn with the natural oils retained.

deer drive — People moving noisily with the intent of driving deer toward a hunter, who is positioned in a strategic spot, at a point, draw, or well-traveled path.

Dept. of Game and Fish — See *Game and Fish Dept.*

diamond willow — (*Salix*) Willow that grows in moist places. It was used for making local hand-designed furniture, but is now relatively scarce. The tree has rough bark and is characterized by diamond shapes left on the trunk at the base of lower branches, which have sloughed off.

dog sled — Non-rigid sled to avoid breakage on the trail. The uprights were braced and held in place with moose hide thongs. The handle bars were attached in the same manner which allowed for a slight movement. My dog team sled, built in this manner by Art Smith and pulled first by dogs and then by snowmobile has lasted 50 years.

dog team — Three to seven dogs which were trained to pull, were driven in a single line with whipple trees from their harnesses attached to a single rope. They were controlled by commands understood by the lead dog: *Mush* - to go; *Gee a little* - about 45° right; *Haw a little* - about 45° left; *Gee* - hard right; *Haw* - hard left; *Gee back* - reverse self on right side; *Haw back* - reverse self on left side.

Egi — See *Malamute, Siberian.*

eiderdown — Large sleeping bag with water resistant canvas on the outside, a wool liner inside. The filling was down of the eider duck, until the ducks became scarce, and use of their down was prohibited.

esker — A ridge of gravel and sand formed by a subglacial stream.

feather (the paddle) — Turn the paddle blade parallel with the water as it is swept forward.

fire line — Ahead of where the fire is expected to go, watering or cutting a strip on the ground to stop a ground fire.

fire towers — Tall manmade watch towers topped with an enclosed platform. The towers were manned to spot forest fires early. The fire tower system was replaced with an air patrol.

fish box — Wood box constructed especially for commercial packing and shipping of fish. Resorts also used it for packing their customers' fish.

flesh — To remove the fat and meat from a hide.

flint — Stone material capable of starting a fire.

flintlock gun — Gunlock in which a flint is used to ignite the powder in the pan. Voyageurs carried flint from France, but found streaks of flint imbedded in rock on the north shore of Gunflint Lake, which they used to replenish their supply.

floating bog — Wet and spongy floating ground made up of closely compacted bushes whose root systems are largely in the water.

forest service — Federal or state department which oversees logging, tree planting and fire fighting.

frost holes — Spots in the ground which are almost bottomless during spring thaw. Result from frost going particularly deep.

fur sales — International fur sales take place with the New Year and again in spring. Winnipeg, Montreal and New York are the centers of greatest activity.

Game and Fish Dept. — Minnesota state conservation officials. Now named Department of Natural Resources (DNR).

game wardens — Enforcement personnel of Game and Fish Dept. who, at this time, spent their days in the field.

gasoline lantern — Camp-type lantern runs on pressure, so it requires frequent pumping, and its mantles are extremely fragile.

Gee — Dog team command. See *dog team.*

grease burn — Grease left on a beaver hide after skinning will burn the hide, causing it to become brittle and of little value.

ground — A single telephone line must have a wire from the telephone attached to a stake driven in the ground, serving as a completed electrical impulse.

hardpan — Soil mixture of clay and fine gravel that compacts like cement.

Haw — Dog team command. See *dog team.*

headdress, feathered — Adornment worn by Indian men during their dances to display their finery.

head waters — Spring or creek that culminates in a river or lake.

hew – To cut a groove in a log or to smooth one side of a log with an axe.

hide – Animal's skin with fur, but with all fat, meat and grease removed.

hide needle – Curved steel needle about three inches long having a large eye. Used to sew a beaver hide to an ash hoop with meter line.

hide stretcher – Two elongated thin pieces of wood shaped in the form of the hide to be stretched. After the cleaned hide is put on the stretcher, a tapered wedge is inserted. When the hide has dried the wedge is pulled out, and the hide can be removed. Different size stretchers are used for ermine, mink, fisher, fox, otter and wolf.

ice chisel – Narrow chisel with a long handle used to make a hole through the ice.

ice harvest – Task of sawing ice cakes from the lake, hauling and stacking them in the ice house to store for the summer.

ice house – Small building close to the lake filled with ice cakes and insulated with sawdust to keep the ice for summer.

ice roads – Logging roads were made slippery by pouring water in the ruts, which froze and allowed sledges of logs to be pulled out of the woods by horses.

ice saw – Saw with wide teeth, similar to a crosscut saw except the teeth are larger and the handle is a crossbar. Used for cutting ice in the lake.

ice tongs – The tongs used to pull ice from the water had a long hinged handle attached to teeth which hold the ice. Short-handled tongs were used to carry smaller cakes to the ice box.

Indian charms – Hung from a tick-a-noggin. Circular and laced like a spider web to catch evil spirits.

Indian pipe – (*monotropa unifora*) Leafless saprophytic plant.

kenoggin – Term used by some Indians instead of tick-a-noggin. When pronounced, the first sound "tick" is very soft, and in some cases dropped.

kerosene lamp – Lamp with a wick and chimney; burns kerosene.

limb – To saw or chop all the limbs from a felled tree before cutting the trunk into lengths.

loggers – Men who cut, limbed and skidded logs to a staging area.

logging – Harvesting of trees and hauling them to a logging area for transportation – by river, lake or truck.

logging camp – A complete camp – kitchen, dining hall and bunk houses set up for loggers to stay in the woods where they were working.

long johns – woolen underwear extending the full length of the body.

Magnetic Rock Trail – Two and a half mile hiking trail leading to a 40-foot rock left standing on end by the glacier. The rock deflects the needle of a nearby compass.

Malamute, Siberian – A large dog used in the far north for pulling sleds. There is no hair between the toes on their foot pads, an advantage when traveling in wet snow or slush. Malamutes do not bark, but howl, and they are a little larger build than huskies.

maul — A heavy long-handled mallet with a head made of steel.

metallic circuit — Telephone circuit having two lines: one acting for transmission and the other serving as a return ground. Much more efficient than a single wire.

meter line — A heavy tough string used by commercial fishermen to make and repair fish nets. We bought our meter line from fishermen in Grand Marais.

miners — Men who came as prospectors and attempted to find a paying seam of ore.

minnow trap — Elongated wire trap with a funnel-shaped opening on each end. Baited with bread and submerged in a beaver pond.

moccasins — Foot covering worn by Indians, made from moose hide or deer hide. Usually short with a cloth top for winter.

mosquito bar — (mosquito net) A fine mesh gauze was referred to as a "bar." It barred the mosquitoes from approaching.

mukluks — Foot covering made from moose hide that extends high on the leg. Winter moccasins.

North Lake Portage — One of three land portages along the international boundary waters. Also the height of land separating the Hudson Bay and Lake Superior watersheds.

Norwegian Elkhound — A robust dog of Norwegian origin with a thick grey coat and a broad head.

oakum — tarred group of hemp fibers used for caulking seams.

"one lunger" — A single cylinder gasoline engine.

outhouse — See *biffy.*

packstraps — Adjustable shoulder straps attached to a packsack.

packsack — A large water resistant canvas pack carried on the back by attached shoulder straps and used to carry clothes, food or equipment on a trip. Consists of one large compartment with a buckled flap covering the top opening.

parch — To cook slightly and partially dry the rice so the outer coating can be removed.

parka — A large hooded outer garment worn in winter for warmth and a wind break. Insulated with wool or down, and the hood is often faced with wolf fur (which frosts very little from a person's breath) or wolverine fur (which frosts not at all).

peat bog — Marsh with an accumulation of partially-carbonized vegetable matter, predominately mosses.

peat moss — Decayed vegetable matter found in a peat bog.

peeled logs — On the better cabins the bark is removed with a draw knife, because an unpeeled log cannot be scribed and fitted closely. When logs are peeled, they last ages. Most trapper cabins were built without removing the bark from the logs.

personal gear — Bare essentials needed for travel — extra socks, compass, axe, matches, extra shirt.

192

pitch — Sap from spruce or balsam trees was heated and applied to seams of birchbark canoes to seal them. Spruce gum is sometimes chewed, and also is used as a poultice to heal an infected wound.

pole bed — Bed in a trappers shack with a frame covered with poles about three inches in diameter.

poplar — Common name used for the trembling aspen found in our woods.

portage — Trail over which travelers carry canoes and goods around non-navigable waters or from one lake to another.

Precambrian period — The earliest period, in geological time — during the formative years of the earth.

privy pads — Seat pads used in winter made from a heavy material and kept in the warm house. When it was necessary to go to the outside toilet the warm pad was placed around the frosty hole.

Quetico Provincial Park — Canadian park that borders the Boundary Waters Wilderness Area.

quirt — Short-handled riding whip with a rawhide lash.

road head — Road that ends at a lake or a hiking trail.

root cellar — Underground cellar used for storing potatoes, canned goods and non freezable articles. The interior temperature remained at about 40° F year-round.

rough peeling — Removing the outer rough bark with an axe and leaving the inner bark to be removed with a draw knife.

runner — A sled runner made of birch or ash wood. An iron strap was often attached to the underside of the runner for endurance.

runway — Water trail made by beaver from their house, or to the shore, where they have cut and dragged out limbs of poplar trees for their food storage pile.

rutting season — Yearly breeding season for moose and deer, usually in late October to early November.

St. Paul Winter Carnival — An ice carnival staged for a week each winter in St. Paul, Minnesota.

saw, crosscut — A large-toothed saw for cutting timber by hand. If used singly it had a single handle similar to a hand saw, and the saw was about five feet long. If two sawyers worked together, a seven-foot double saw was used, and it had upright handles at each end.

scent, fox — Artificial odoriferous scent used in trapping to attract fox; other scents are used for other animals.

Shebandowan Reservation — Canadian reservation near Lake Lac des Mille Lac. The Indians had to go to Shebandowan to collect their treaty money of $5.

shirttails — Wool shirts (boys' or men's) with tails were commonly worn. Often two shirts and a wind break (light jacket) were used. The top shirt could be added or removed depending on temperature change or activity undertaken.

skin rough — Skinning the animal before fleshing the hide.

sledge — Sled used for transporting logs on ice roads.

slush ice — Gooey unfrozen mixture of water and snow encountered on lakes in winter. It is created when water seeps to the ice surface through a crack and stays covered by a thick layer of snow, keeping the slush from freezing.

snapping trees — In very cold weather, like 30 below, due to moisture within the wood, the trees emit a snapping sound.

snares — Traps made by looping a special type of wire that is hung over a trail. The animal is caught by the neck and killed.

snow blindness — Temporary blindness caused by the reflection of the sun on snow. The inflammation is very painful and lasts for several days.

snowmobiling — Traveling on lakes and over portages with a gasoline-powered vehicle which has rubber tracks at one end and skis at the other.

snowshoes — The frame of Indian snowshoes is two pieces, joined at both ends. The Maine shoe has a one-piece frame bent at the top, which is what we used, but the Indians made me several pair of their style which I also used. Other styles are Pickerel shoes, long and very narrow, which were used by a few trappers, and Bear Paw, which are round, with no tail. They were used by foresters cruising timber.

snowshoe rabbits — (*Lepus americanus*) Large hare with furry feet that allow it to travel on snow. The coat is grey brown in the summer and white in the winter.

sphagnum moss — Moss which grows more than two feet thick in swamps. It was used for insulation in ice houses and for packing fish.

spruce root — Root of a spruce tree. The more slender roots were gathered by the Indians, split and used to sew baskets and birchbark seams.

spud bar — Long bar with a chisel-like end tapered on both sides. Used to jar loose a sawed cake of ice from the field.

square-stern canoe — A 17' or 18' canoe with a foot cut off the stern and replaced with a square end for a small outboard motor.

squaw wood — Dried poplar found on a beaver house; any dry sticks.

stagged-trousers — Pants chopped off to the desired length with an axe.

Star route — Mail route that comes to a dead end.

stern paddler — Person who paddles from the rear of the canoe and who controls its direction. One person traveling by canoe sits in the stern.

stone hammer — Large square-headed hammer with a long handle, used for splitting rocks.

tag alder — (*alnus*) A high bush whose stems are sometimes used to make beaver hoops. Not very strong and does not hold a shape well.

tepee — Circular Indian tent held up by a series of poles that meet at a central point. Covering could be birch bark or blankets.

tick-a-noggin — Indian cradleboard. A baby is wrapped in blankets and laced snugly to the backboard. A protective head loop in the shape of an M is attached to the top of the board. The depression in this loop is built to fit under a mother's arm so the baby can be nursed without being removed from its "nest."

toboggan — Our toboggans were eight to 10 feet long with the width of a snowshoe trail. They were so limber that they would snake across low windfalls.

tom-tom — Primitive drum made of raw hide. Tapped with a baton-like stick or with hands.

topping — Forest fire rolling at great speed from treetop to treetop.

trapline — An established area apportioned to one trapper who had built several trapping shacks six or eight miles apart. He then set up and maintained trapping lines between these cabins as he snowshoed from one to the other. He was careful not to overtrap the game, so he would have a continuous yearly yield.

trappers — People who came into the region to trap animals for the value of their furs.

trappers' cabins — Small cabins scattered along a trapline at one-day snowshoeing intervals. Each cabin was completely equipped with stove, sleeping bag and food.

trapping trails — Trails established by the Indians that led through valleys from one lake to another and were used for generations.

tump line — A strap extending from the top of a packsack to the top of a person's head. Tump lines were also attached to the sides of a canoe to help distribute the weight over a long portage and were often used on tick-a-noggins.

Twin Cities — Minneapolis-St. Paul, Minnesota.

voyageurs — The first white-man trapper-traders to travel the boundary waters.

water hole — A hole chiseled through the ice to obtain water for drinking and washing. Marked with a stick — covered to slow refreeze.

Webster-Ashburton Treaty — Treaty giving the rights to both Canadians and Americans to travel the portages along the international waterway regardless of which side of the border the portage was located on.

wheel dog — The dog hitched next to the sled; next in importance on the team to the lead dog.

wild rice — (*Zizania aquaticica*) Grain that grows in shallow lakes; the rice-like seeds were a staple for the Indians.

Wilderness Express — Two passenger busses operated during WWII by Don Brazell from Duluth to the end of the Gunflint Trail. As one bus came up the Trail the other bus went down.

windfalls — Dead trees blown down by the wind.

Windigo — An Indian spirit connected with a wind strong enough to snap branches from trees.

winnow — To free rice grain from the chaff by flipping it in the air from a basket and catching it again repeatedly. Only done when a gentle wind is blowing; the breeze blows the chaff away, and the grain drops back in the basket.

wood borers — Insect that bores holes in wood, working under the bark of dry trees.

195

INDEX

196

WANT TO ORDER THIS BOOK?
OR OTHERS?

Use this form to order copies of *Woman of the Boundary Waters*, or other titles by Women's Times Publishing:

___ **WOMAN OF THE BOUNDARY WATERS**
   by Justine Kerfoot
   Canoeing, Guiding, Mushing and Surviving
   ISBN 0-910259-03-8   200p, cloth, $14.95

___ **KIDS' NORTHWOODS ACTIVITY BOOK**
   by Jane Lind, illustrations by Liz Sivertson
   Innovative nature activities for ages 5-12. Great for
   canoe or camping trip. Glossary, 3-color pencil set.
   ISBN 0-910259-06-2   26p, spiral, $4.95

___ **INGEBORG'S ISLE ROYALE,** by Ingeborg Holte
   Memories of family life in a commercial fisherman's
   family in the early 1900s, on the "incomparable
   Island," now a national park.
   ISBN 0-910259-01-1   95p, paper, $7.95

___ **I WALK ON THE RIVER AT DAWN,**
   poems by Joanne Hart, drawings by Betsy Bowen
   Poems of Winter
   ISBN 0-910259-05-4   38p, paper, $5.95

___ **IN THESE HILLS,** poems by Joanne Hart
                   drawings by Jayne Gagnon
   Collection of poems and drawings of Grand Portage,
   Minnesota — Reservation, home of Grand Portage
   Chippewa Band
   ISBN 0-910259-04-6   22p, paper, $3.75

- -

Please add $1.50 for first book, 50¢ for each add'l book to cover
mailing costs. Minnesotans please add 6% sales tax.

To: Women's Times Publishing, Box 215, Grand Marais, MN 55604

Name _____

Address _____

City_____State_____ Zip_____

Prices subject to change without notice.
Bulk purchase inquiries invited.